SpringerBriefs in Entrepreneurship and Innovation

SpringerBriefs in Entrepreneurship and Innovation focus on the nexus between entrepreneurship and innovation from an interdisciplinary and international perspective. Of particular interest are volumes that emphasize, for example, alternative interpretations and extensions of current thought about entrepreneurial and innovative processes, critiques of and proposals for public policies aimed toward an improved culture for entrepreneurship and innovation, entrepreneurship and innovation and the generation of knowledge, and international comparisons of dimensions of entrepreneurial and innovative activity.

SpringerBriefs present concise summaries of cutting-edge research and practical applications across a wide spectrum of fields. Featuring compact volumes of 50 to 125 pages, the series covers a range of content from professional to academic. Typical topics might include:

- A timely report of state-of-the art analytical techniques
- A bridge between new research results, as published in journal articles, and a contextual literature review
- A snapshot of a hot or emerging topic
- An in-depth case study or clinical example
- A presentation of core concepts that students must understand in order to make independent contributions.

Briefs are characterized by fast, global electronic dissemination, standard publishing contracts, standardized manuscript preparation and formatting guidelines, and expedited production schedules.

Alberto Onetti · Alessia Pisoni

Open Innovation in Action

Models, Metrics, and Use-Cases for Corporate-Startup Collaboration

Springer

Alberto Onetti
Department of Economics
University of Insubria
Varese, Italy

Alessia Pisoni
Department of Economics
University of Insubria
Varese, Italy

ISSN 2195-5816 ISSN 2195-5824 (electronic)
SpringerBriefs in Entrepreneurship and Innovation
ISBN 978-3-032-17331-7 ISBN 978-3-032-17332-4 (eBook)
https://doi.org/10.1007/978-3-032-17332-4

This Springer imprint is published by the registered company Springer Nature Switzerland AG
The registered company address is: Gewerbestrasse 11, 6330 Cham, Switzerland

Preface

In 2025, talking about Open Innovation requires a completely different approach. The concept, coined by Henry Chesbrough more than 20 years ago, remained largely confined to academia for its first decade. Between 2010 and 2020, most large companies began experimenting with it, followed—more hesitantly—by mid- and small-sized enterprises. Today, Open Innovation has become mainstream: almost universally recognized as the "new" way of driving research and innovation, regardless of industry, geography, or company size.

What was once a black box of exploratory approaches, with little expectation of measurable outcomes, has now matured into a discipline with consolidated models, best practices, and KPIs.

That said, implementing Open Innovation successfully is still far from straightforward. While established companies are accustomed to collaborating with external providers, engaging with startups and scaleups is a very different game. The cultural clash between structured organizations and fast-moving (and sometimes fast-failing) ventures is anything but trivial. Moreover, innovation takes time. And the real impact of Open Innovation—beyond new products or technologies—often lies in less tangible outcomes: strategic market intelligence, cultural transformation, and enhanced reputation. These dimensions are difficult to capture through traditional metrics and KPIs, especially in the short to medium term.

In this book, we have sought to distill the lessons learned from analyzing hundreds of companies across sectors, sizes, and geographies—organizations that have started, scaled, evolved, reshaped, or even abandoned their Open Innovation journeys. Our aim is to help corporate executives design, refine, and adapt their own strategies; identify the models that best fit their needs; understand the organizational and cultural conditions required; and, ultimately, track and measure results in a meaningful way. For startup and scaleup founders and CXOs, we also provide a behind-the-scenes glimpse into how established corporates think and operate when engaging with smaller, newer ventures.

In 2025, there are no more alibis for not innovating. And there is no doubt that Open Innovation is the only way forward. It is not easy, but it is no longer optional. The cost of failing to evolve is clear. And it is called company survival.

Like ships crossing turbulent waters, companies must learn to sail alongside smaller, faster vessels—sometimes lifeboats, sometimes torpedoes—whose course will ultimately shape their own journey. Evolve or be extinct.

Varese, Italy

Alberto Onetti
Alessia Pisoni

Acknowledgments First and foremost, the authors would like to express their sincere gratitude to **Mind the Bridge** for granting privileged access to data and sharing invaluable first-hand insights into how companies and startups implement Open Innovation practices in their daily operations. In particular, we deeply appreciated the unique opportunity to draw on the insights from the **Corporate Startup Stars Awards**, an initiative organized since 2015 in partnership with the **International Chamber of Commerce (ICC)**.

We are equally grateful to all the corporate executives, founders, entrepreneurs, and CXOs with whom we have had the pleasure of collaborating over the past decade. Countless hours spent discussing, experimenting, and learning together have shaped this work. The Open Innovation journeys of their companies have been a constant source of inspiration, without which this book would not have been possible.

This publication also benefitted from the inspiring and stimulating discussions during the **2025 "Oxford in Varese" Residence Week for Entrepreneurship Scholars**. Parts of this work were presented at the **World Open Innovation Conference** held in San Francisco in 2018, as well as at numerous events, summits, and workshops around the globe.

Last but not least, we owe very special thanks to our mixed research "crew" at **University of Insubria/Mind the Bridge**: Serena Valente, Giorgio Di Fiore, Max Brigonzi, and Emanuele Aversa.

We were also fortunate to receive the kind and professional support of Nitza Jones **(Springer)** throughout the publication process.

Note: The book has been jointly written by Alberto Onetti and Alessia Pisoni. Specifically, Alberto Onetti wrote the Preface, Chapter 4 and the Conclusions. Alessia Pisoni wrote the Introduction, Chapter 2, 3 and 5.

Competing Interests The authors declare to have no competing interests.

Praise for *Open Innovation in Action*

"Open innovation really has grown up, since its inception more than 20 years ago now. This book provides the latest insights into the concept, both in theory and especially in practice. If open innovation interests you, I strongly advise you to check out this book!!"

—Henry Chesbrough, *UC Berkeley-Haas and Luiss University, Rome*

Contents

About the Authors

Alberto Onetti Full Professor of Entrepreneurship and Management at the University of Insubria and Adjunct Professor at IE Business School. A recognized global thought leader in Open Innovation (LinkedIn Top Voice), he currently serves as Chairman of Mind the Bridge, a San Francisco-based global innovation advisory platform. In this role, he has supported numerous multinational corporations in designing and executing Open Innovation programs—including Venture Client, Venture Builder, Intrapreneurship, and Corporate Venture Capital initiatives. In 2014, Alberto was selected by the European Commission to lead the Startup Europe Partnership, the first integrated Open Innovation platform aimed at supporting the growth and sustainability of the European startup and scaleup ecosystem. In 2025, he was appointed by the European Commissioner for Startups, Research and Innovation Zaharieva to join the Task Force responsible for defining the EU Startup and Scaleup Strategy.

Alessia Pisoni Associate Professor of Innovation Management at the Department of Economics, University of Insubria of Varese. She holds a Ph.D. in Economics of Production and Development with a dissertation on the German Corporate Governance Model. Thereafter, her research interests spanned from Business Strategy to Entrepreneurship and Innovation Management. With the aim to enrich her cultural and academic experience, she has been visiting scholar (research and teaching) in several universities/colleges and research institutions around Europe and overseas. She also regularly participates in international conferences to share insights on her research. Since inception she has been part of the scientific committee of the Research Centre of Innovation and Life Science Management, for which she has coordinated several research projects focused on High-Tech/Green Technologies. Since 2010, she has also been collaborating with Mind the Bridge research activities focused on open innovation (corporate-startup collaboration) and tech startup/scaleup ecosystems. Nowadays, her research interests are in the area of entrepreneurship, innovation and internationalization.

About the Authors

Abbreviations

BU	Business Unit
CEO	Chief Executive Officer
CIO/CInO	Chief Innovation Officer
CVC	Corporate Venture Capital
CXO	Chief-level executive (generic)
EBITDA	Earnings before Interest, Depreciation and Amortization
HR	Human Resources
ICT	Information and Communication Technologies
KPI	Key Performance Indicator
LP	Limited Partner
M&A	Merger and Acquisition
OI	Open Innovation
PoC	Proof of Concept
PoV	Proof of Value
R&D	Research and Development
ROI	Return on Investment
TVPI	Total Value to Paid-In Capital
VC	Venture Capital

Chapter 1
Introduction

Abstract How to turn open innovation into action is the leading question the book tries to answer by providing evidence from theory and practice. Drawing on nearly two decades of combined academic and practitioner experience in Entrepreneurship and Open Innovation, the Authors aim to offer readers a comprehensive, 360-degree perspective on the topic. This book serves as both a practical guide for managers looking to implement Open Innovation strategies and an authoritative reference for scholars conducting research in the field.

Keywords Open innovation · Competition · Disruption

1.1 Introduction to Open Innovation

Today, Open Innovation has become mainstream, both in terms of industries involved and its geographical reach. The fear of missing opportunities, combined with a growing awareness of the potential benefits of collaborating with innovative and agile businesses, has driven an increasing number of large companies to engage in this evolving field. In a fast-paced world, we are witnessing incumbents from the "old economy" losing market shares and traction, while startups emerge as key drivers of the "new economy". No company—regardless of size, industry, or geography—is immune to disruption.

Open Innovation has evolved from being the research interest of a few into a mainstream academic field. Initially developed within the domain of technology and innovation management, it is now frequently cited in strategy, general management, and organizational behavior journals. Since the seminal contribution of Henry Chesbrough (2003), a significant body of research has emerged, and the field has continued to evolve (Radziwon & Chesbrough, 2024). Open Innovation is widely acknowledged as a "distributed innovation process" (Chesbrough, 2003, 2006), grounded in the "purposively managed knowledge flows across organizational boundaries" (Chesbrough & Bogers, 2014, p. 17).

A. Onetti and A. Pisoni, *Open Innovation in Action*,
SpringerBriefs in Entrepreneurship and Innovation,
https://doi.org/10.1007/978-3-032-17332-4_1

As even Chesbrough himself acknowledges, "models do evolve", and in many cases, practice advances faster than theory. The key contribution of this book lies in providing a fresh, up-to-date, and practice-driven perspective on how large corporations are implementing Open Innovation today, with a particular focus on startup collaboration and the most recent, real-world best practices.

With the aim of bridging the gap between theory and practice, this book addresses three main issues:

- Why is Open Innovation essential for incumbents to face disruption, and why is it particularly relevant in today's competitive scenario?
- How can corporates and startups mutually benefit from Open Innovation activities?
- Which models and tools are adopted to implement Open Innovation initiatives, and what challenges arise during their implementation?

In exploring these questions, we provide evidence from the latest trends and real-world case studies, highlighting best practices in corporate-startup collaboration. As practitioners involved in innovation and startups for decades, we are also aware of the "short shelf life" of this book. Nevertheless, we embrace this challenge and strive to capture the current state of the art as accurately as possible.

1.2 Overview of the Book Structure

Combining insights from nearly two decades of scholarly research on Open Innovation with practical experience, the book offers a comprehensive, 360-degree perspective on how to translate Open Innovation into action.

The Introduction provides an overview of the book's structure and its main objectives.

The Second Chapter introduces the reader to the field of Open Innovation by focusing on the benefits of its implementation by corporates. It highlights how corporate-led Open Innovation activities have evolved significantly over the past decade, driven by accelerating industry disruption, shorter life cycles, and the growing recognition of the value of collaborating with innovative, agile startups.

Chapter Three represents the core of the book, examining the concrete actions adopted by leading companies to collaborate effectively with startups. In addition to internal Open Innovation strategies and processes, the chapter outlines the various forms these initiatives take, linking them to specific innovation goals and the company's stage of Open Innovation maturity.

The Fourth Chapter analyzes the most recent trends in corporate-startup collaborations and provides insights from case studies showcasing how leading companies implement Open Innovation and how their approaches have evolved over time. Specifically, it explores the emerging models of corporate-startup collaboration, with a focus on hybrid strategies and challenges involved in their implementation.

The Fifth Chapter deals with the mechanisms and metrics needed to fully capture the benefits of Open Innovation adoption by companies. As outlined, comprehensive measurement systems and KPIs are still at an early stage of development.

Concluding remarks and implications for scholars and practitioners complete the work.

References

Chesbrough, H. (2003). *Open innovation: The new imperative for creating and profiting from technology*. Harvard Business Press.

Chesbrough, H. (2006). *Open business models: How to thrive in the new innovation landscape*. Harvard Business Press.

Chesbrough, H., & Bogers, M. (2014). Explicating open innovation: Clarifying an emerging paradigm for understanding innovation. In H. Chesbrough, W. Vanhaverbeke, & J. West (Eds.), *New frontiers in open innovation* (pp. 3–28). Oxford University Press.

Radziwon, A., & Chesbrough, H. (2024). Open innovation as a field of knowledge. In H. Chesbrough, A. Radziwon, W. Vanhaverbeke, & J. West (Eds.), *The Oxford handbook of open innovation* (pp. 3–18). Oxford University Press.

Chapter 2
Turning Startup Collaboration into Competitive Advantage

Abstract The chapter aims at introducing the reader into the Open Innovation field of research by specifically focusing on the benefit of Open Innovation implementation by corporates. As the next chapter will clarify, corporate-led Open Innovation activities have evolved significantly over the past decade. Evidence from recent studies on companies listed among the Fortune Global 500 shows how industry disruption is accelerating, and competitive cycles are shortening. The fear of losing opportunities, together with an increased awareness of the potential benefits of collaborating with innovative and agile businesses (i.e., startups), has encouraged a growing number of large companies to engage in Open Innovation activities.

Keywords Incumbent · Startup · Collaboration · Competitive advantage · Fortune Global 500

2.1 Why Open Innovation Is Key to Corporate Survival

Since the original Open Innovation definition proposed by Chesbrough in 2003, research has evolved considerably, expanding both in scope and depth to encompass a broader array of actors, organizational settings and innovation practices (Chesbrough et al., 2024).

The original definition of Open Innovation as "an emergent model of innovation in which firms draw on research and development that may lie outside their own boundaries" (Chesbrough, 2003) through "inflows and outflows of knowledge [allowing] to accelerate internal innovation and expand the market for external use of innovation" (Chesbrough, 2006) was further strengthened after a decade of research in the volume by Chesbrough and colleagues published in 2014. Accordingly, Open Innovation was defined as a "distributed innovation process" [...] "based on purposively managed knowledge flows across organizational boundaries, using pecuniary and non-pecuniary mechanisms in line with the organization's business model" (Chesbrough & Bogers, 2014, p. 17). Consistently, the Open Innovation model bridges two sides of the innovation process: the "inbound flow", involving the acquisition and

A. Onetti and A. Pisoni, *Open Innovation in Action*,
SpringerBriefs in Entrepreneurship and Innovation,
https://doi.org/10.1007/978-3-032-17332-4_2

integration of externally generated ideas into the focal organization, and the "outbound flow", which refers to the transfer of ideas, knowledge, resources or talented people to external organizations. To succeed firms should leverage both internal and external avenues for creation and commercialization (Chesbrough, 2003, 2006). Coupled processes combine inbound and outbound knowledge flows and entail "co-creation with (mainly) complementary partners through alliances, cooperation, and joint ventures during which give and take are crucial for success" (Enkel et al., 2009, p. 313). Cross-industry collaborations, i.e., the transfer of knowledge from one industry to another, have gained relevance in a variety of contexts (Enkel & Gassmann, 2010), thus suggesting that innovation advantages can also arise from the heterogeneity of the partners involved in the process.

The considerable amount of literature published in the Open Innovation field over the past two decades provides now a richer perspective on innovation processes (Bogers & West, 2024; Radziwon & Chesbrough, 2024; West & Bogers, 2014). External knowledge flows from startup and universities/research centers, alongside external sources of funding such as venture capital and corporate venturing, have gained paramount importance, as Chesbrough and colleagues also argued in the recently published "Oxford Handbook for Open Innovation" (2024). In this book, the "increasingly dispersed nature" of R&D in the innovation process is discussed (Radziwon & Chesbrough, 2024, p. 19). As recently pointed out by Chesbrough (2024, p. 9) "Open Innovation scope extends beyond any single innovation process [...] it is a more general process involving the creation and management of purposive knowledge flows across organizations".

New perspectives for studying Open Innovation approaches have broadened to include additional levels of analysis—both intra- and inter-organizational (Audretsch et al., 2023; Bogers et al., 2017; Dahlander et al., 2016; West, 2014)—as well as new research objects such as ecosystems, platforms (Nambisan et al., 2018; Radziwon et al., 2017) and digital technologies/infrastructures (Autio et al., 2024). Recent contributions also show a renovated scholarly interest in the business outcomes of Open Innovation (Chesbrough, 2020).

It is understood that the fast-pace of technological change and the complex nature of technologies drive the fact that only few organizations can nowadays afford to maintain in-house knowledge and expertise in every potentially relevant area (Chesbrough et al., 2014; Chesbrough & Crowther, 2006; Van Lieshout et al., 2021). A highly complex business environment requires corporations to continuously improve their innovative capabilities. To respond to changing market conditions and remain competitive with more agile companies, corporations are urged to increase their adaptability, flexibility, and creativity.

2.2 Corporate-Startup Collaboration as Key Driver of Success

As a matter of fact, startups are driving major innovations that are disrupting industries from the bottom up. The growing concern over missed opportunities, coupled with an increased recognition of the strategic value of engaging with innovative startups, has led an increasing number of large, established companies to explore and invest in this once-unfamiliar territory.

Corporate-led Open Innovation activities have changed considerably over the last decade. Research on corporate-startup interactions has increasingly attracted the attention of both scholars and practitioners, focusing on identifying the various strategies and models that corporates adopt to engage with the startup community (Chesbrough, 2003, 2012, 2020; Weiblen & Chesbrough, 2015) and the factors that made such collaboration successful (Minshall et al., 2010; Weiblen & Chesbrough, 2015). Rather than perceiving startups solely as a source of disruption, companies are increasingly seeking to collaborate with them as a catalyst for corporate innovation.

Corporate-startup engagement in the tech industry takes a huge variety of forms (Weiblen & Chesbrough, 2015). These are traditionally classified into outside-in and inside-out modes of Open Innovation. More specifically, outside-in startup programs aim at "making existing startups' technology accessible and useful for the sponsoring corporation", while inside-out platform startup programs aim to "promote and establish the use of the corporation's technical platform by other businesses" (Weiblen & Chesbrough, 2015, p. 72).

As Chesbrough and colleagues argue, there is "no single best model for engagement", the model to be adopted depends on the industry and on the goals that companies want to achieve through the engagement (Chesbrough, 2024; Lu & Chesbrough, 2022; Weiblen & Chesbrough, 2015). In an effort to avoid disruption, large corporates have increasingly looked for ways to adopt more entrepreneurial approaches. As argued, traditional models such as corporate venture capital (CVC) or internal accelerators are now complemented by more agile and faster means to engage with the startup community (Weiblen & Chesbrough, 2015). The next Chapter will illustrate more in detail the most recent trends identified in respect to modes of collaboration.

Collaboration between corporates and startups, if done properly, can bring considerable benefit to both. However, large, established corporation and startups are intrinsically different from one-another. Large, established corporations are assumed to have resources, bargaining power and the ability to leverage economies of scale. On the other side, startups[1] are "experiments", i.e., new business projects with a strong commitment to innovation, organizational agility and marked ambitions of growth.

[1] According to one of the most widely used definitions, coined by Steve Blank, a startup is "a temporary organization used to search for a repeatable and scalable business model" (Blank, 2010, 2013). The scalability is to be considered as the crucial aspect of this definition (Onetti, 2014). This company model is usually associated with levels of capital requirements that go beyond the self-financing capacity of the founders. Consequently, in the early stages, startups base their scale-up on third-party funding. The development of the product or service and its placing in the market pass through a period (longer or shorter, depending on the characteristics of technologies and on

2.3 Open Innovation to Stay Competitive

Innovation has long been a key driver of competitive advantage for companies. In today's globalized economy—characterized by rapid technological change, digitization and shorter product life cycle—Open Innovation has become a cornerstone for corporate strategy. As recently shown by the "Open Innovation Barometer",[2] 95% of corporations now adopt Open Innovation practices, with over half (54%) implementing them for most or all of their projects. This trend highlights the growing pressure on firms to stay agile and the necessity of co-innovating with startups in order to maintain competitiveness and face disruption in a rapidly changing environment.

A recent study conducted by Mind the Bridge shows how between 2000 and today, the Fortune Global 500 index[3]—the list of the world's largest companies by revenue—has undergone a dramatic transformation (Mind the Bridge, 2024). Of the companies ranked in 2000, only 41% still remain on the list (Fig. 2.1). The others have been replaced, indicating that industry disruption is accelerating and competitive cycles are shortening. In other words, 3 out of 5 global incumbents have been displaced or commonly said "disrupted" (Mind the Bridge, 2023, 2024). The study analyzes approaches and modes of corporate-startup collaborations based on the "Gold Standard Open Innovation Framework" developed by the International Chamber of Commerce and Mind the Bridge (Mind the Bridge and ICC, 2022). Given that modes of collaboration are in continuous evolution, data are regularly updated to capture the newly emerging approaches to Open Innovation.[4] The proposed framework evaluates how companies adopt and implement Open Innovation practices to drive growth and adaptability. Using this framework, the Fortune Global 500 index of corporate global leaders are classified into two categories (Mind the Bridge, 2024)[5]:

- *Open Innovation Leaders*: these companies adopt a comprehensive and holistic approach to Open Innovation, effectively implementing a range of tools and practices aligned with the "gold standards" identified. They account for 41.6% of the Fortune Global 500. Notably, this proportion closely mirrors the percentage of companies that have remained in the index since 2000. While no direct correlation between these data points has been established, it suggests exploring whether a

target markets) characterized by large investments and no revenues or, in any case, revenues that are insufficient to cover the expenses. Fundraising is designed to bring startups along the phases marked by "negative burn" until the time when they will generate cash (becoming "cash flow positive").

[2] The "Open Innovation Barometer"—powered by the Economist Impact—is a survey-based research program, conducted by Economist Impact and sponsored by SUSE, studying openness in innovation processes. Available at: https://impact.economist.com/projects/open-innovation/

[3] The Fortune Global 500 (https://fortune.com/ranking/global500/) ranks the largest 500 corporations worldwide as measured by total revenue.

[4] See Mind the Bridge and ICC (2022) and Mind the Bridge (2024) for further insights on the methodology.

[5] The analysis does not include entities such as state-affiliated enterprises operating under planned economy structures.

Fig. 2.1 The journey of the companies listed in the Fortune Global 500. *Source* Own elaboration adapted from (Mind the Bridge 2024)

broad Open Innovation strategy contributes to sustained inclusion in the Fortune 500 over time;

- *Open Innovation Challengers*: these companies are currently exploring Open Innovation through a limited range of tools in a relatively unstructured and opportunistic way, rather than as a part of a structured strategy. They account for 38.6% of the Fortune Global 500.

In recent years, corporates have accumulated extensive experience in collaborating with startups across a variety of initiatives and tools. They range from Intrapreneurship Programs, Accelerators, Startup Studios and Venture Builders, to Innovation Outposts/Antennas in global tech hubs, partnerships (the so-called, Venture Client), investments and acquisitions. As the next chapter will detail, tools and initiatives that corporates employ to engage with startups are multiple and continuously evolving over time. For this reason, they are constantly monitored to adapt to mutating conditions and trends as well as internal strategy and structure.

References

Audretsch, D. B., Belitski, M., Caiazza, R., & Siegel, D. (2023). Effects of open innovation in startups: Theory and evidence. *Technological Forecasting and Social Change, 194*, 122694. https://doi.org/10.1016/j.techfore.2023.122694

Autio, E., Hameri, A. P., & Legenvre, H. (2024). Open technology maneuvering in digital infrastructures. In H. Chesbrough, A. Radziwon, W. Vanhaverbeke, & J. West (Eds.), *The Oxford handbook of open innovation* (pp. 505–518). Oxford University Press.

Blank, S. (2010). What's a startup? First Principles. http://steveblank.com/2010/01/25/whats-a-startup-first-principles.

Blank, S. (2013). Why the lean start-up changes everything. *Harvard Business Review, 91*(5), 63–72.

Bogers, M., & West, J. (2024). A multi-level framework for selecting and implementing innovation modes. In H. Chesbrough, A. Radziwon, W. Vanhaverbeke, & J. West (Eds.), *The Oxford handbook of open innovation* (pp. 65–88). Oxford University Press.

Bogers, M., Zobel, A. K., Afuah, A., Almirall, E., Brunswicker, S., Dahlander, L., Frederiksen, L., Gawer, L., Gruber, M., Haefliger, S., Hagedoorn, J., Hilgers, D., Laursen, K., Magnusson, M.

G., Majchrzak, A., McCarthy, I. P., Moeslein, K. M., Nambisan, S., Piller, F. T., Radziwon, A., Rossi-Lamastra, C., Sims, J., & Ter Wal, A. L. (2017). The open innovation research landscape: Established perspectives and emerging themes across different levels of analysis. *Industry and Innovation, 24*(1), 8–40. https://doi.org/10.1080/13662716.2016.1240068

Chesbrough, H. (2003). *Open innovation: The new imperative for creating and profiting from technology*. Harvard Business School Press.

Chesbrough, H. (2006). *Open business models: How to thrive in the new innovation landscape*. Harvard Business School Press.

Chesbrough, H. (2012). Open innovation: Where we've been and where we're going. *Research-Technology Management*, *55*(4), 20–27. https://doi.org/10.5437/08956308X5504085

Chesbrough, H. (2020). *Open innovation results: Going beyond the hype and getting down to business*. Oxford University Press.

Chesbrough, H. (2024). A reconsideration of open innovation after 20 years. In H. Chesbrough, A. Radziwon, W. Vanhaverbeke, & J. West (Eds.), *The Oxford handbook of open innovation* (pp. 3–18). Oxford University Press.

Chesbrough, H., & Bogers, M. (2014). Explicating open innovation: Clarifying an emerging paradigm for understanding innovation. In H. Chesbrough, W. Vanhaverbeke, & J. West (Eds.), *New frontiers in open innovation* (pp. 3–28). Oxford University Press.

Chesbrough, H., & Crowther, A. K. (2006). Beyond high tech: Early adopters of open innovation in other industries. *R&D Management, 36*(3), 229–236. https://doi.org/10.1111/j.1467-9310.2006.00428.x

Chesbrough, H., Radziwon, A., Vanhaverbeke, W., & West, J. (Eds.). (2024). *The Oxford handbook of open innovation*. Oxford University Press.

Chesbrough, H., Vanhaverbeke, W., & West, J. (Eds.). (2014). *New frontiers in open innovation*. Oxford University Press.

Dahlander, L., O'Mahony, S., & Gann, D. M. (2016). One foot in, one foot out: How does individuals' external search breadth affect innovation outcomes? *Strategic Management Journal, 37*(2), 280–302. https://doi.org/10.1002/smj.2342

Enkel, E., & Gassmann, O. (2010). Creative imitation: Exploring the case of cross-industry innovation. *R&D Management, 40*(3), 256–270. https://doi.org/10.1111/j.1467-9310.2010.00591.x

Enkel, E., Gassmann, O., & Chesbrough, H. (2009). Open R&D and open innovation: Exploring the phenomenon. *R&D Management, 39*(4), 311–331. https://doi.org/10.1111/j.1467-9310.2009.00570.x

Lu, Q., & Chesbrough, H. (2022). Measuring open innovation practices through topic modelling: Revisiting their impact on firm financial performance. *Technovation, 114*, 102434. https://doi.org/10.1016/j.technovation.2021.102434

Mind the Bridge. (2023). Open Innovation: The Age of Hybridization and Results—Evolve or Be Extinct. https://mindthebridge.com/2023-open-innovation-evolve-or-be-extinct/

Mind the Bridge. (2024). The Open Innovation Imperative. Adapting to stay competitive—Insights from the Fortune Global 500. https://mindthebridge.com/the-open-innovation-imperative-adapting-to-stay-competitive-evolve-or-be-extinct-season-2024/

Mind the Bridge and ICC. (2022). Gold standards for the world's companies to incorporate open innovation and corporate-startup collaboration—Best practices for worldwide companies and SMEs emerging from corporate startup stars awards. https://mindthebridge.com/2022-open-innovation-gold-standards/

Minshall, T., Mortara, L., Valli, R., & Probert, D. (2010). Making "asymmetric" partnerships work. *Research-Technology Management*, *53*(3), 53–63. https://doi.org/10.1080/08956308.2010.11657631

Nambisan, S., Siegel, D., & Kenney, M. (2018). On open innovation, platforms, and entrepreneurship. *Strategic Entrepreneurship Journal, 12*(3), 354–368. https://doi.org/10.1002/SEJ.1300

Onetti A. (2014). Scaleups. When does a startup turn into scaleup?. https://startupeuropepartnership.eu/

Radziwon, A., Bogers, M., & Bilberg, A. (2017). Creating and capturing value in a regional innovation ecosystem: A study of how manufacturing SMEs develop collaborative solutions. *International Journal of Technology Management*, *75*(1–4), 73–96. https://doi.org/10.1504/ijtm.2017.10006145

Radziwon, A., & Chesbrough, H. (2024). Open innovation as a field of knowledge. In H. Chesbrough, A. Radziwon, W. Vanhaverbeke, & J. West (Eds.), *The Oxford handbook of open innovation* (pp. 3–18). Oxford University Press.

van Lieshout, J. W., Van Der Velden, J. M., Blomme, R. J., & Peters, P. (2021). The interrelatedness of organizational ambidexterity, dynamic capabilities and open innovation: A conceptual model towards a competitive advantage. *European Journal of Management Studies, 26*(2/3), 39–62. https://doi.org/10.1108/EJMS-01-2021-0007

Weiblen, T., & Chesbrough, H. (2015). Engaging with startups to enhance corporate innovation. *California Management Review, 57*(2), 66–90. https://doi.org/10.1525/cmr.2015.57.2.66

West, J. (2014). Challenges of funding open innovation platforms: Lessons from Symbian Ltd. In W. Vanhaverbeke, J. West, & H. Chesbrough (Eds.), *New frontiers in open innovation* (pp. 29–49). Oxford University Press.

West, J., & Bogers, M. (2014). Leveraging external sources of innovation: A review of research on open innovation. *Journal of Product Innovation Management*, *31*(7), 814–831. https://doi.org/10.1111/jpim.12125

Chapter 3
The Corporate Guide to Open Innovation

Abstract As seen, Open Innovation has evolved over time. Alongside internal Open Innovation strategies and processes, leading companies implement concrete Open Innovation actions that result in effective collaboration with startups. The Chapter outlines the diverse forms through which these actions are implemented according to the innovation goal to be reached and the stage of development along the company's Open Innovation journey.

Keywords Collaboration · Models and tools · Enabling factors · Open Innovation journey

3.1 The Open Innovation Framework: Models, Tools, and Enabling Factors

As seen in the previous chapter, the increasing globalization of technology and product development has, over time, eased the implementation of Open Innovation. Advances in information and communication technologies (ICT) have also reduced spatial distances enabling innovation processes to become more open and connected than ever before (Siota et al., 2020).

In recent years, large established corporations have accumulated significant experience in collaborating with startups and scaleups across various initiatives and tools (Gassmann et al., 2010; Mind the Bridge, 2022; Onetti, 2021a). At the same time, companies have increasingly placed Open Innovation at the center of their strategies and organizational structures, creating the conditions needed for effective collaboration with startups.

Figure 3.1 illustrates both dimensions of this Open Innovation Framework.

On the left side of the chart, we have positioned the models, tools, and initiatives that corporates deploy to engage with startups and scaleups—typically the most visible aspects from outside the organization.

A. Onetti and A. Pisoni, *Open Innovation in Action*,
SpringerBriefs in Entrepreneurship and Innovation,
https://doi.org/10.1007/978-3-032-17332-4_3

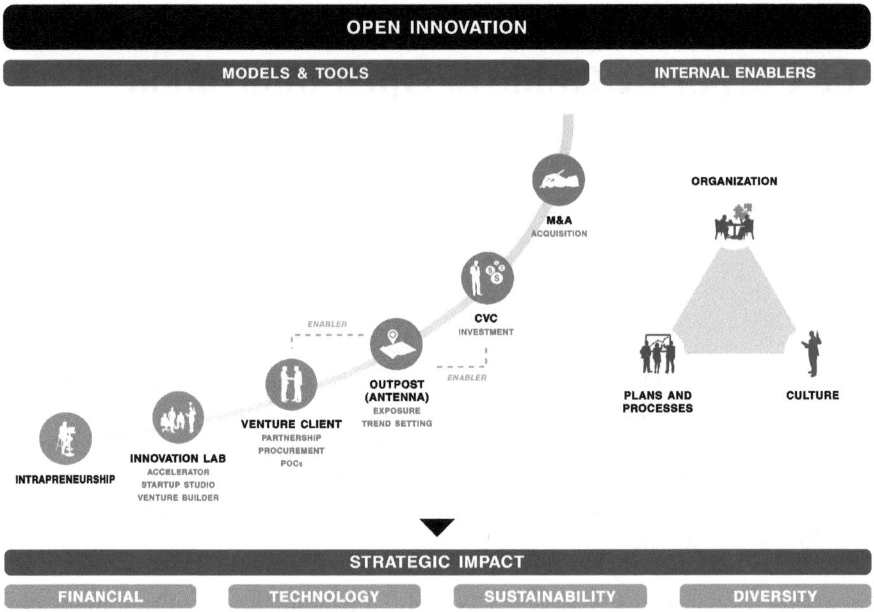

Fig. 3.1 Open Innovation Framework: tools and enablers. *Source* Own elaboration adapted from Mind the Bridge (2024a)

On the right side, by contrast, we have mapped the internal enabling conditions—such as strategy, organization, processes, and corporate culture—that, while less visible, are equally critical to achieving sustainable innovation outcomes.

In the following pages, the multiple complementary approaches and modes targeting different goals and innovation horizons are illustrated.

3.1.1 Models and Tools

As illustrated in Fig. 3.1, models and tools of interaction between corporates and startups can take many forms and shapes ranging from Intrapreneurship, Accelerators, Startup Studios and Venture Builders (jointly referred to as Innovation Labs), Outposts/Antennas in global tech hubs, partnerships (so-called Venture Client), investments (CVC), and acquisitions and acqui-hires (M&A). Activities are presented in the following and ranked according to the resource commitment required (from low to high).

Intrapreneurship Programs

Launched with the goal of stimulating an entrepreneurial mindset among employees, intrapreneurship is a bottom-up innovation approach that enables corporations to harness their employees' creativity to generate corporate innovations (Antoncic &

Hisrich, 2001; Bosma et al., 2013; Neessen et al., 2019). Since the seminal contributions of Pinchot (1985) and Drucker (1986), a variety of synonyms have been introduced by scholars to describe the concept of intrapreneurship. Among these, the most widely used is "corporate entrepreneurship" (Amo, 2010; Burgers & Covin, 2016; Urbano et al., 2022). As scholars also pointed out, entrepreneurship includes both the creation of new companies and entrepreneurial activities within existing organizations (Antoncic & Hisrich, 2001; Parker, 2011). According to Neessen and colleagues, "the intrapreneur is not a single actor within the environment but acts as part of an organization and will thus be influenced by it" (2019, p. 565). Regardless of the terminology used, recent years have seen a growing interest in the study of "intra-entrepreneurship" activities (Hernández-Perlines et al., 2022). Literature has mainly explored the link between intrapreneurship and business performance (Zahra, 1991), innovation (Sinha & Srivastava, 2013) and organizational effectiveness (Neessen et al., 2019). As suggested, further research should focus on the peculiarities of entrepreneurial development within different organizations (Hernández-Perlines et al., 2022).

Intrapreneurship initiatives are typically structured around calls for ideas—either periodic (e.g., annual) or continuously open—and progress through multiple stages and gates (below is an example of a common intrapreneurship program structure, Fig. 3.2). At the initial stage, a relatively broad pool of projects and ideas is assessed, with participants provided access to resources and tools to refine and elaborate their proposals. Through one or more subsequent stages, a narrower subset of projects advances to receive tailored support, professional mentorship, and preparation for pitching to top management. Ultimately, implementation—often also via dedicated internal venture building initiatives—is reserved for those projects that demonstrate clear value creation and tangible impact.

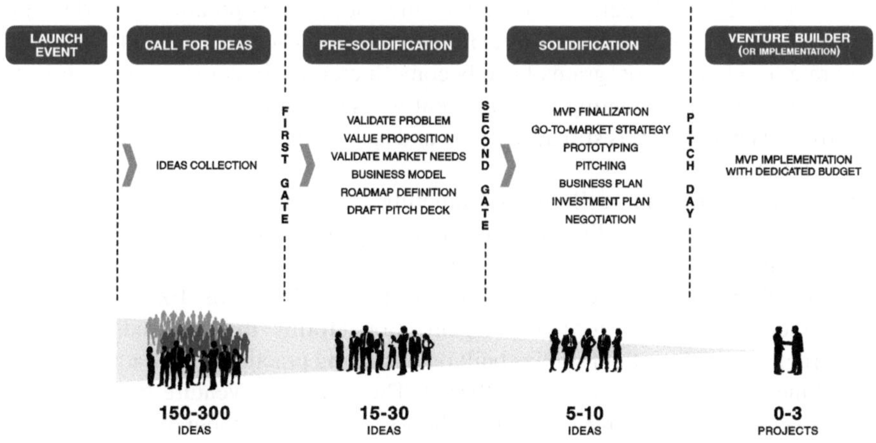

Fig. 3.2 Stage-Gate process of intrapreneurship programs. *Source* Own elaboration adapted from Mind the Bridge (2025a)

Recent trends indicate that innovation leaders are increasingly restructuring their internal idea-generation programs to move beyond purely HR-driven educational objectives and reposition them as initiatives designed to generate deal flow (Mind the Bridge, 2023a, 2024a; Onetti, 2021a). Consequently, such programs are typically managed by the corporate Innovation Unit rather than the HR department. Another notable development (Mind the Bridge, 2025a) is the progressive decline in the number of applications once a program has been in place for several years. This phenomenon appears to be linked, on the one hand, to internal saturation—data suggest that it is difficult to engage more than 5–10% of the employee base—and, on the other hand, to decreasing engagement over time. After the "honeymoon effect" of the initial editions, sustaining employees' interest becomes more challenging. In response, some programs have begun to incorporate external contributions from entrepreneurs and startups, while others are increasingly adopting corporate venture builders to further develop and scale the most promising projects emerging from their intrapreneurship initiatives.

Innovation Labs

Companies employ different schemes to engage with early-stage startups. Corporate Accelerator programs—among the earliest models introduced—are increasingly being complemented, or in some cases replaced, by Venture Builders and Startup Studios, which provide a smaller number of carefully selected projects with more intensive, hands-on support.

The "traditional" Corporate Accelerator models are structured programs that offer established companies promising avenues to explore new ideas and drive innovation. These short-term initiatives support cohorts of startups (also known as "batches") —either physically or virtually—by providing key resources such as co-working space, funding, mentorship, and networking opportunities to scale their business (Cohen et al., 2019; Kohler, 2016). On the other side, the corporation gained insight into the startup's technology and entrepreneurial talents (Seitz et al., 2024). Although corporate acceleration programs have become increasingly common, most organizations are still experimenting with different ways of setting up and managing their initiatives. The literature is still developing and lacks a clear framework (Cohen et al., 2019; Qin et al., 2019).

In this context, Venture Builders (sometimes referred to as Corporate Venture Builders—CVB) are rapidly emerging as a way for corporations to "build their own startups". There's not yet a definite way of defining a Venture Builder in the literature (Belingheri & Lechner, 2025) as well as in the praxis. Extant definitions and characterizations refer to "hybrid organizational forms" that are rapidly emerging from practice and from field studies built on observing practitioners (Baumann et al., 2018; Onetti, 2021a, 2021b, 2021c, 2021d). The Corporate Venture Builder goal is to create new businesses from scratch, in-house, and support them in scaling. Extant evidence highlights the structured process that enables the simultaneous scaling of multiple ventures.

Startup Studios are organizations—often referred to as "startup factories"—relying on external collaboration with entrepreneurs to co-create startups. They not only provide managerial support but also act as founders (the so-called "Founder Model") and co-founders ("Co-Founder Model"). Startup Studios' primary objective is to create as many startups as possible, focusing on the rapid scalability of a small number of initiatives. In doing so, they rely on external investors.

Distinguishing among the different models of Innovation Labs is not straightforward, as these approaches are relatively recent and continue to evolve. Venture Builders, as corporate-driven initiatives, tend to be more strategically oriented: their primary objective is to develop ventures aligned with the corporation's strategic priorities, which are ultimately transferred to the relevant business units. Accordingly, both management and funding are predominantly internal.[1] Similar to Venture Builders, Startup Studios adopt a highly selective approach, concentrating on a limited number of initiatives, whereas Corporate Accelerators typically pursue a broader portfolio strategy, primarily aimed at providing exposure to innovative early-stage solutions. Further details are provided in Table 3.1.[2]

Venture Client

BMW Startup Garage[3] pioneered the Venture Client model. In 2015, BMW was seeking a new approach to collaborate with startups and consequently boost corporate innovation (Gimmy et al., 2017). This way, a company becomes a client of the startup (typically later-stage), providing crucial validation beyond revenue. It purchases a first unit of a startup's product, service or technology (procurement), but does not receive equity. The eventual outcome is to scale the relationship from an initial pilot/ proof of concept (PoC) to a full deployment and broader commercial relationship.

What differentiates this approach from traditional procurement is the engagement process with startups, which occurs through iterative steps as part of a structured scouting process. A recent study confirms how the Venture Client is the most used tool to engage with startups (Mind the Bridge, 2024a, 2024b). Corporates increasingly adopt systematic scouting frameworks to evaluate and filter large numbers of startups. In a typical Venture Client funnel for a large established corporation, an initial long list of approximately 1000 to 2500 startups per year is generated, but only a limited subset—around 20 or more annually—progresses to long-term collaborations (Fig. 3.3). Before full industrial integration, solutions are generally validated through pilots (also referred to as PoC or as Proof of Value—PoV). The ultimate goal of a Venture Client is to generate impact on the P&L in the mid-term through partnership with startups and scaleups. The evaluation of the impact of Venture Client initiatives involves several dimensions, such as generating new revenue streams, achieving cost-savings through process efficiency, shortening time-to-market (Mind the Bridge, 2024b). However, these indicators are challenging to measure, particularly in the short term (Gutmann & Lang, 2022).

---

[1] See: https://sifted.eu/articles/venture-builders-type and https://sifted.eu/articles/venture-builders-downturn-brnd

[2] See: https://sifted.eu/articles/venture-builder-characteristics

[3] See: https://www.bmwgroup.com/en/innovation/open-innovation/startup-garage.html

Table 3.1 Accelerators, Startup Studios, and Venture Builders

	Accelerator	Startup studio	Venture builder
Number of ventures	Many Work with large groups/ cohorts of startup	Few Launch a few initiatives per year	Few Launch a few initiatives per year
Origination	External Work with pre-existing early-stage startups	Internal Build from concept/ scratch	Internal/ external Build from concept or ideas coming from top management, employees or outside entrepreneurs/startups
Corporate control	Partial Corporate sponsors the program and eventually defines the challenges	Minimal Corporate might invest in some startups	Full Corporate decides which ventures to start
Corporate ownership	Minority Corporate-eventually-invests into startups participating in the program	Minority Corporate might invest into startups launched by the studio, majority taken down the way through M&A	Majority Ventures are controlled by corporate since day one
Management of ventures	External Venture is independent, corporate might eventually invest-seed mostly, growth capital eventually	External Venture created and run by an external entity, corporate might eventually invest—seed and growth capital	Internal Venture run internally with support from outside
Funding	Mostly external Corporate might contribute to seed/early-stage funding	Mostly external Seed funding provided by startup studio, corporate might join to support growth and/or exit	Mostly external Seed and growth capital provided by corporate
Outcome	An indipendent startup	A startup to be exited in 3–5 years	A new business to be handed over to business unit or spin-off company (participated by corporate)
Goal	Exposure to early-stage solutions	Acquisition (eventual) of externally developed solutions	Launch of new business

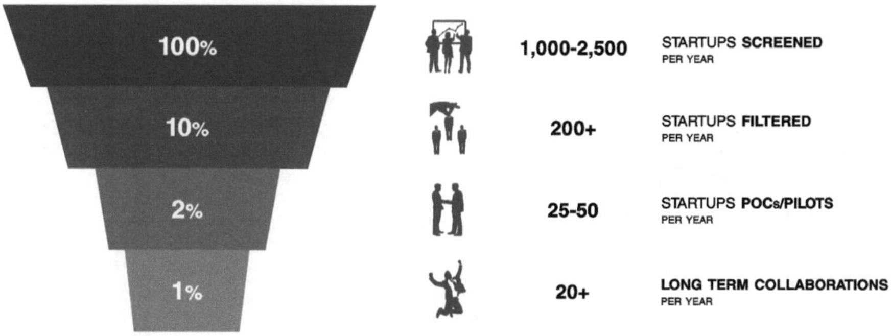

Fig. 3.3 The Venture Client model: Typical Funnel. *Source* Own elaboration adapted from Mind the Bridge (2024a)

In this respect, Venture Client is described as a "win-win" situation (Nesta, 2015). For startups, securing a corporate client can be a pivotal step toward industrial validation, stability, and scale. For corporates, procurement offers to onboard validated innovations more deeply inside the organization or integrate them into supply chains for the benefit of end-users. However, as mentioned in the previous chapter, such partnerships require a more collaborative mindset and a thorough rethinking of procurement processes.

Innovation Outposts

To access the latest technology trends and expand their engagement with startups, corporates are increasingly establishing a presence—through Innovation Outposts—within a global innovation ecosystem (Brouthers et al., 2022). Innovation and scaleups tend to cluster in a few main hotspots, with Silicon Valley remaining the premier destination for corporates seeking to stay at the forefront of innovation (see Fig. 3.4, which provides a comparative ranking of the world's major technology ecosystems).

Innovation Outposts serve as strategic hubs, enabling corporations to embed themselves in local ecosystems to scout cutting-edge technologies, engage with startups, and pursue new business opportunities through venture client development, investments, and M&As (Decreton et al., 2021; Mind the Bridge, 2016; Onetti, 2021a; Stenholm et al., 2018). Empirically exploring how corporates engage dynamic entrepreneurial and innovation ecosystems reveal four primary types of open Innovation Outposts, each designed to support specific innovation objectives. These include Antennas and Corporate Venture Capital (CVC) Offices, Innovation Labs and more structured R&D Centres (Mind the Bridge, 2022, 2023a, 2024a, 2024d).

Specifically, a Corporate Innovation Antenna is a "lean setup" within a global innovation ecosystem, sometimes supported by a local bridging organization. It typically consists of a small team focused on trendspotting and engaging with startups at an individual level. The Antenna's role is to identify emerging innovation trends and help the company R&D department and other business units gain exposure to the

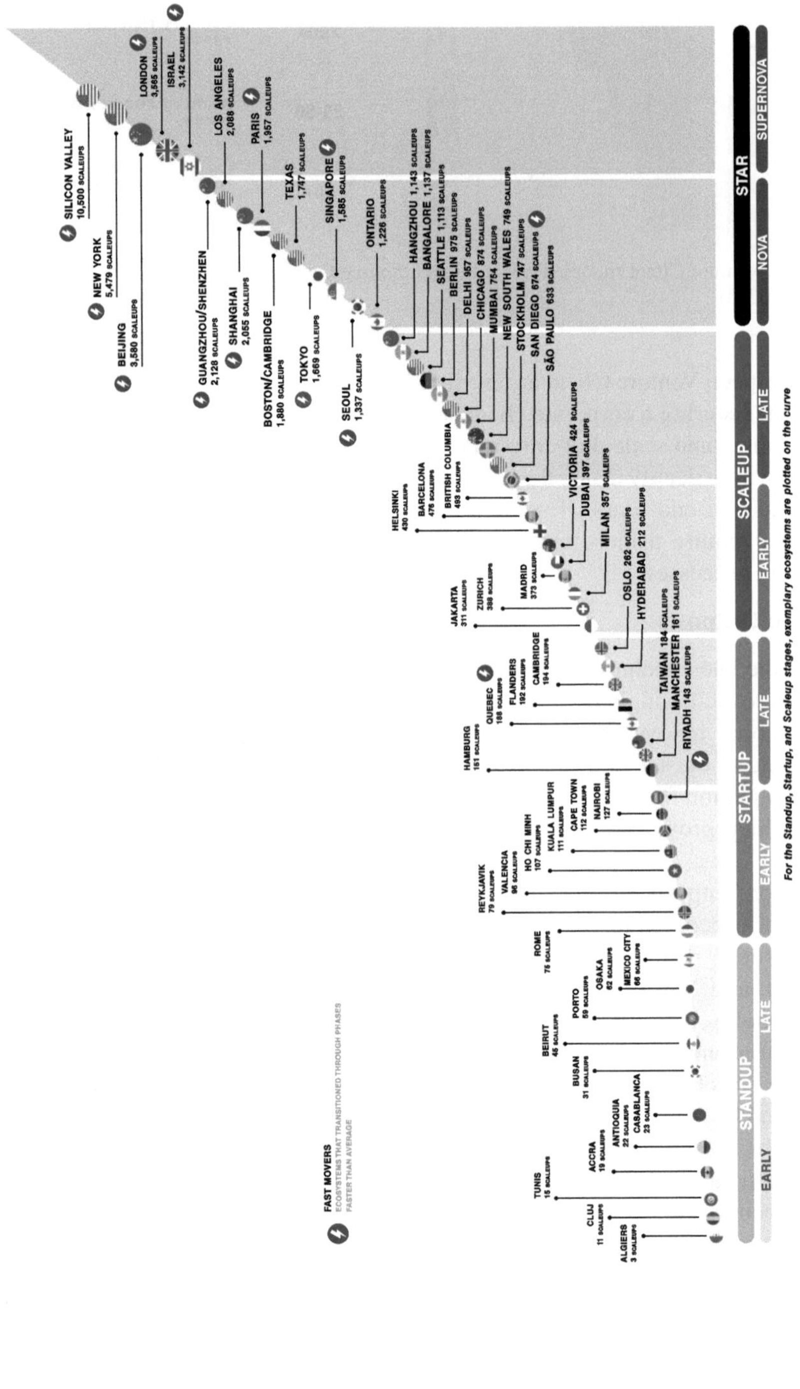

Fig. 3.4 World's innovation regions on the innovation ecosystems life cycle curve. *Source* Own elaboration adapted from Mind the Bridge (2024c)

latest technologies and business models. It often serves as the first step toward establishing a larger corporate presence in the ecosystem. Large multinational corporations frequently set up multiple antennas across different emerging tech hubs. Corporate Venture Capital (CVC) Offices are corporate venture capital funds based within the ecosystem to pursue startup investments and strategic partnerships. Like Antennas, CVC Offices are typically small teams, usually comprising fewer than 10 people. A Corporate Innovation Lab is an outpost that functions as an incubator/venture builder/accelerator, leveraging corporate resources to conduct external technology research and development. It represents a leaner version of a traditional corporate R&D facility and enables closer interaction with startups developing new technologies. Last but not least, a Corporate R&D Center represents a well-established presence, typically employing between 50 and 1000 people. These centers leverage local startup technology and talent to provide corporates with new solutions. Some large multinational corporations set up multiple R&D centers, each specializing in different technologies.

As of March 2024, over 400 open Innovation Outposts had been mapped in Silicon Valley alone—which remains the premier destination for corporates seeking to stay at the cutting edge of innovation—involving companies from more than 20 industries, including electronics, biotechnology, finance, and banking (Mind the Bridge, 2024d, 2023b). This industry diversity highlights the value of open Innovation Outposts, namely, securing access to new technologies and remaining at the forefront of industry advancements. A significant portion of these outposts are hybrid structures integrating activities typical of different outpost typologies. More recently, South Korea and Israel have also emerged as two of the most thriving global innovation ecosystems. This growing relevance is reflected in the rising number of open Innovation Outposts established in these regions (82 in South Korea and 224 in Israel), which serve as strategic bridges between local ecosystems and global corporate innovation networks (Mind the Bridge, 2023c, 2023d).

Corporate Venture Capital

A common way for corporates to engage in entrepreneurial activity is to finance it (Dushnitsky & Lenox, 2005, 2006). The practice of investing in startups is commonly referred to as Corporate Venture Capital-CVC (Chesbrough, 2002; Chesbrough & Tucci, 2004; Gutmann et al., 2023).

There are different ways to categorize CVCs (Fig. 3.5). One possible framework considers two key dimensions: the investment horizon (ranging from close to core to ahead of business) and the value creation objective (strategic vs. financial).

There are two main schools of thought when it comes to CVC investment horizons (Sauvage et al., 2022). The first argues that CVCs should stay close to the core business. These teams tend to focus on Horizon 1 investments—sustaining and incremental innovation. Often referred to as Evolutionary Innovators, their mandate is to support the existing business and strengthen current capabilities. For some companies like Salesforce, Microsoft, and Qualcomm, which thrive on third-party companies building on their platforms, this CVC approach also serves to nurture and expand their ecosystems—hence they are labeled Ecosystem Builders. The second view sees the CVC arm as a strategic function that should operate with greater independence,

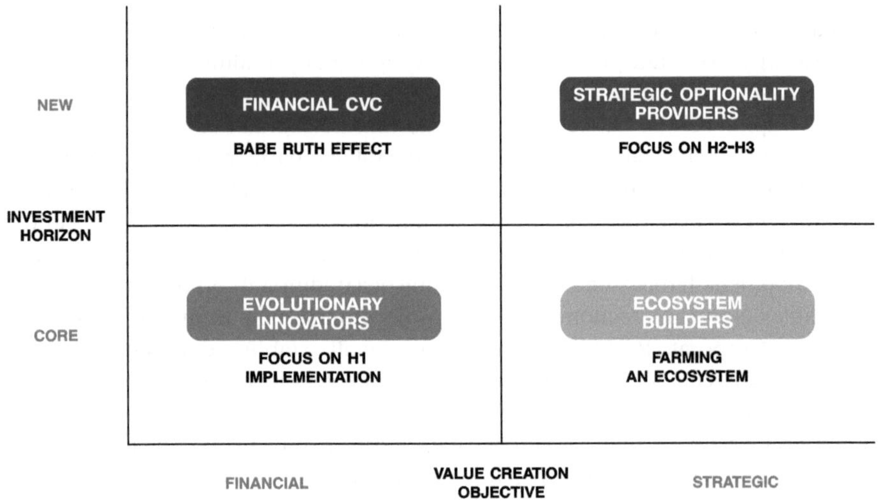

Fig. 3.5 CVC Categories. *Source* Own elaboration based on the literature review

investing ahead of the business in Horizon 2 and 3 opportunities—adjacent markets and disruptive innovations. These CVCs aim to create strategic optionality for the parent company and are often called Strategic Optionality Providers.

One of the biggest problems with investing close to the core business is that you can't really change the shape of the mothership (or disrupt the parent company). CVCs shouldn't be used for safe bets and financial returns. A CVC's financial returns, whatever the magnitude, are unlikely to be material for the success of the parent company. The ultimate return on innovation investment is survival. In this regard:

- CVCs are supposed to be the "eyes and ears" of the parent company and report back to the mothership the strategic insights gained from scanning potentially disruptive trends and anticipating external change.
- They should take bets on innovation and test new businesses on a small scale and in a separate environment.
- They should be looking for disruption rather than investing in something that solves current needs. It makes no sense to ask for advice from business lines. They will give you a shopping list in short term, adjacent innovation, and tell you what they need today or tomorrow. What is needed further beyond that is of little interest, and if it is disruptive, it will be seen as a threat.
- They don't need to invest in startups to have them working with their business units. For that, there is the Venture Client model (proof-of-concept projects and partnerships) that has proven to be able to provide quick strategic wins. And it is faster to deploy.

Corporate venture investments can adopt different models depending on the desired level of involvement and structural setup. Companies may create a dedicated vehicle or a Standalone Fund, invest directly off-balance sheet or participate as Limited Partners (LPs) in third-party managed funds.

A Standalone Fund is a dedicated investment vehicle, either a separate fund or a legal entity, created by a corporation to invest in startups. It can take several forms: (i) a Single LP structure, where the corporation is the sole investor; (ii) a Multiple LP model, where other investors contribute capital but the founding corporation remains the anchor; (iii) a Joint Venture Fund, where the company co-founds and leads a venture capital fund; and (iv) a Multi-Corporate Fund, where several companies co-invest under third-party management, typically reducing strategic control.

Corporates may invest in startups without establishing a dedicated fund or legal entity (Off-balance sheet), adopting different commitment models: (i) an evergreen approach with a multi-year investment budget (the most common); (ii) a single-year commitment limited to the current fiscal year; or (iii) an opportunistic approach based on ad hoc deal evaluations, similar to M&A-driven deal flow.

Last but not least, corporates may also invest in startups as LPs in third-party venture capital funds. The extent to which they can influence the fund's investment strategy and decisions largely depends on the size of their contribution (with anchor partners typically having a stronger voice). Although investment decisions remain externally managed, this model provides visibility into deal flow and is often used either as an entry point into a CVC strategy or as a complement to direct investments, expanding access to specific sectors or geographies.

Standalone Funds offer the most structured approach and enhance visibility in the ecosystem but require substantial capital (often more than $250 M). Off-balance sheet investments are the most adopted model (Strebulaev & Wang, 2021), providing a more flexible alternative suitable for starting to explore potential acquisitions. However, without a fund-like structure, corporates risk slow execution, missed deals, and reputational issues unless backed by a clear long-term vision. Participation in third-party VC funds enables access to market intelligence and deal flow with minimal internal effort, potentially also feeding Venture Client or M&A activities. However, it offers limited influence over investment decisions and lower strategic returns (Mind the Bridge, 2025b).

As more corporates engage in CVC, competition to identify and partner with the right startups has intensified (Siota et al., 2020). Consequently, companies are seeking to enhance the value proposition they offer in their investment activities. An emerging trend shows that some companies are spinning off their CVC arms to create independent funds, also removing any visible affiliation with the parent company (Mind the Bridge, 2025b). The strategic drivers include faster decision-making, fewer conflicts of interest, more market standard compensation structures, the ability to relocate to the top global innovation hubs, greater fundraising flexibility, and the possibility to pursue bolder investment strategies, including the option to invest also in emerging competitors.

M&A

A startup acquisition might complete the innovation journey in case of strong strategic fit. Through the acquisition of the startup, the corporation secures control over the project along with its associated assets. When the corporation acquires the startup primarily to secure talent and human resources (Boyacıoğlu et al., 2024), who are then required to continue working with the acquiring company, the term used is "acqui-hire" (a combination of "acquire" and "hire"). In the past two decades, this practice has emerged as a novel acquisition practice among technology firms with the main goal of accessing startup human capital (Siota et al., 2020).

Beyond the so-called "killer acquisitions" (Cunningham et al., 2021) aimed at inhibiting future competition, scholars argue that startup acquisitions typically do not hinder competition, even when the result in discontinuing the startup's product or service. In recent decades, there has been a marked rise in startup acquisitions by established firms mainly with the purpose of acquiring technology/technological know-how, or of extending product life cycle, or of entering a new market (Brueller & Capron, 2021; Kim, 2022). Post-acquisition challenges have also been taken into consideration in the literature due to substantial organizational differences between the target startup and the acquiring incumbent (Brueller & Capron, 2021). Moreover, empirical evidence shows how geographical and spatial distance is particularly significant in cross-border transactions, i.e., acquirers of startups, both from Europe and the USA, prefer to buy local companies (Mind the Bridge, 2024e; Pisoni & Onetti, 2018). Two primary mechanisms have been identified to mitigate integration challenges in startup acquisitions: early interaction between the acquirer and the target in the form of "strategic alliances", or corporate investments, which provide incumbents with insights into the startup's technology and emerging market (Brueller & Capron, 2021). Summarizing, collaboration between startups and incumbents can generate value well before an acquisition takes place and can also shed light on the best timing for the acquisition to take place (Pisoni & Onetti, 2018) and on the stages through which the collaborative process evolves (Brueller & Capron, 2021).

Not all of the actions outlined above are, or need to be, pursued by corporates simultaneously or in a linear sequence. For example, some corporates choose not to invest in startups but instead focus on collaborations through the Venture Client model. Many companies have decided not to establish any corporate accelerator program—or have shut down existing ones—while others are not notably active in acquisitions. In other words, there is no "one-size-fits-all" model for Open Innovation; rather, there are multiple evolving approaches to be continually tracked and monitored.

3.1.2 Enabling Factors

Open Innovation doesn't always produce results, as Chesbrough also recently acknowledged (2024). Making corporate-startup collaboration effective is often hindered by significant gaps in work practices, substantial cultural differences, and different organizational speed (Weiblen & Chesbrough, 2015). Open Innovation requires enabling conditions at both the strategic and organizational levels (Enkel et al., 2011).

Open Innovation also depends on internal R&D and business units at many stages of the innovation process (Chesbrough, 2024). Knowledge flows inside organizations may become trapped in specific function/levels or processes. As recently argued by Chesbrough (2024, p. 13), "Open Innovation touches many parts of an innovating organization, and each of these parts must adapt its ways of working before open innovation will yield any meaningful results".

Recent studies indicate that the most successful companies implementing Open Innovation have undergone significant internal changes in processes and practice. These firms demonstrate strong organizational commitment, allocate dedicated resources, and establish clear processes supported by appropriate KPIs to track progress (Gutmann, 2019; Gutmann & Lang, 2022; Mind the Bridge, 2022; Onetti, 2021a). Internal enabling conditions—such as innovation strategy, organizational structure, processes, and corporate culture—play a crucial role in determining the success of corporate innovation initiatives.

As seen, Open Innovation involves "purposefully managed knowledge flows across organizational boundaries" (Chesbrough, 2003, 2006; Chesbrough & Bogers, 2014). In most organizations, the R&D unit assumes a central role in managing and coordinating these knowledge flows. Regardless of internal efficiency, every organization should actively engage with both internal and external knowledge networks and communities (Roschek & Jones, 2024). Recent studies show how R&D has become more open to external collaboration, adopting patterns that mirror lean startup processes (Mind the Bridge, 2024a, 2025c).

The creation of a separate organizational unit dedicated to Open Innovation typically originates within the Innovation/R&D function or the Corporate/Business Development unit (Chiaroni et al., 2011). This configuration—based on the ambidexterity principles (March, 1991; O'Reilly & Tushman, 2004; McGrath et al., 2006)—is seen as the most effective as it prevents Open Innovation from being overshadowed by larger units such as R&D or Engineering/IT, which differ in culture, size, objectives and bargaining power. However, an emerging trend is the integration of Open Innovation (and Digital) with the traditional technology units. This approach brings together all the key innovation actors, those who are in charge of identifying and setting the future directions (Innovation, Digital, R&D) and those who have the means to implement them (Technology/Engineering, ICT). The risks, however, remain those previously outlined.

Ideally, the Open Innovation Unit should oversee and coordinate all the innovation initiatives (Outposts, Intrapreneurship, Accelerator/Venture Builder, Venture Client, CVC, M&A). A strong commitment to Open Innovation is also reflected by the presence of a dedicated C-level executive, such as a Chief Innovation Officer (CIO or CInO) or a Chief Digital Officer (CDO), responsible for leading these efforts. Other typical reporting lines for Open Innovation include the CTO, CFO, and VP Corporate Development or Strategy. It is not unusual for different innovation initiatives to report through different lines (frequent examples are CVCs reporting to the CFO, intrapreneurship to HR). To address this fragmentation, companies might establish an "Innovation Committee", composed of CxOs and Area Directors to share insight and jointly evaluate decisions on startup-corporate collaboration (Mind the Bridge,

2024a). Finally, strong top-level buy-in and continuity in governance are key factors for ensuring that Open Innovation initiatives deliver results.

3.2 The Open Innovation Journey: The Road to Implementation

How do companies turn Open Innovation into practice? Empirical evidence on this topic adopting a longitudinal process perspective is limited (Chiaroni et al., 2010, 2011). Extant knowledge is largely derived from in-depth case studies examining the journey of a single company, thus implying the limitations of country-, industry-, and firm-specific factors (Chiaroni et al., 2011). Only a few attempts have been made to compare multiple-case studies or to cluster Open Innovation implementation processes across industries (Chiaroni et al., 2011; Gassmann & Enkel, 2004).

The rich empirical evidence gathered in 15+ years of Mind the Bridge professional advisory and support activities focused on making corporates and startups collaborate allows us to comment on the managerial and organizational levers firms challenge during the Open Innovation implementation process, with interesting implications for both theory and practice. While case studies will be described in depth in the next chapter, in the following section we aim to depict Open Innovation implementation as a journey.

Leading companies implement concrete Open Innovation actions that result in effective collaboration with startups. By adopting the "Three Horizons" approach developed by McKinsey (Baghai et al., 1999; Curry & Hodgson, 2008), it is possible to identify the activities carried out according to each company's stage of development along its Open Innovation journey. It is worth noting that diverse innovation goals (horizons) require the adoption of different models and initiatives depending on the level of experience a company has developed over time in implementing Open Innovation initiatives/practices (Fig. 3.6). Horizon 1 focuses on innovations with a potential short-term impact on the core business, which need to be pursued alongside adjacent and disruptive innovation in Horizons 2 and 3. That said, the broad range of models and initiatives adopted by large companies should be viewed as a benchmark to be reached over time, with the necessary adjustments and customization dictated by each company's size, industry, and strategic priorities.

Specifically, depending on when companies adopt dedicated Open Innovation strategies and the level of experience they accumulate in implementing them, different types of initiatives tend to emerge (Fig. 3.6). Early-stage companies usually focus on exploratory actions with limited scope, often aimed at gaining exposure and with a primarily local reach. At the other end of the spectrum, companies further along in their Open Innovation journey combine a solid internal organization with hands-on experience and measurable results. They continuously refine their approach by leveraging metrics and streamlined processes. Between these two poles lies a

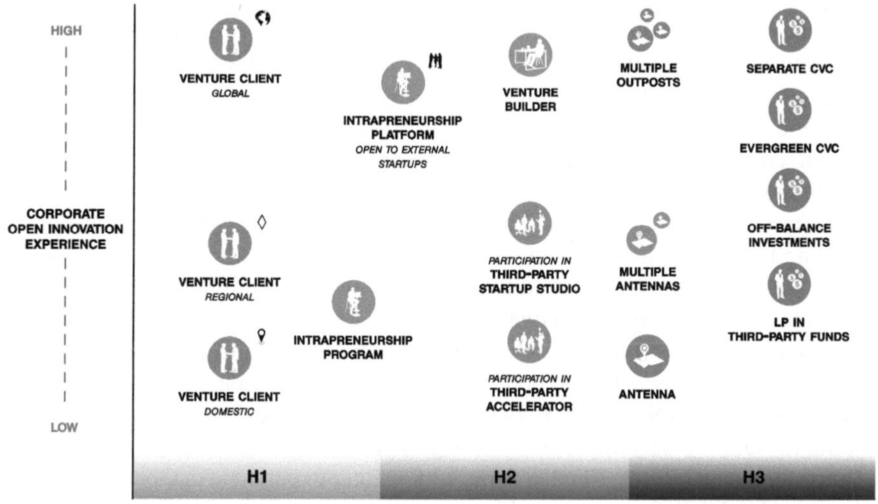

Fig. 3.6 The Open Innovation Tools vs. Stage of Open Innovation journey and horizon. *Source* Own elaboration adapted from Mind the Bridge and ICC (2022)

transitional phase, where companies set the necessary preconditions, articulate a clearer innovation strategy, and begin to design and execute external Open Innovation initiatives. In this stage—characterized by "learning by doing"—firms gradually build experience while still lacking some of the internal conditions required to deliver results consistently.

As stated, different innovation goals (horizons) require the adoption of different tools:

- Horizon 1: The Venture Client model enables the rapid adoption of innovative solutions from startups and scaleups, but—as noted—its effectiveness relies on a structured and selective scouting process. Companies at the early stage of their Open Innovation journey should begin by scouting within their domestic market to avoid cultural and regulatory barriers. This initial focus helps organizations gain exposure to technology trends, test and deploy innovative solutions quickly through pilots and PoCs, and foster a stronger internal culture of innovation and risk-taking. When a company's size, internal innovation culture, and risk attitude allow, the scouting scope can be expanded globally. In this phase, it is often advisable to outsource part of the scouting process to experienced advisory organizations that can provide market knowledge, networks, and expertise for high-quality matchmaking. Technology hotspots with a high density of scaleups—such as Silicon Valley—should be prioritized to maximize results. Establishing a direct presence within these ecosystems, for instance, by setting up an innovation Antenna or Outpost, can significantly enhance scouting effectiveness. Moreover, the Venture Client process should remain highly selective and structured around specific challenges defined by the company's business units' needs. Finally, solutions to these innovation needs can also be identified internally by leveraging employees' capabilities through structured intrapreneurship programs.

- Horizon 2: Launching new businesses in adjacent markets requires early exposure to emerging technologies and business models. This typically involves leveraging tools such as Accelerators, Startup studios, and Venture Builders. However, the effectiveness of corporate-run accelerators has increasingly been questioned, leading to their exclusion from recommended approaches. For companies at the early stage of their Open Innovation journey, joining a third-party accelerator can provide initial exposure to innovative ideas and early-stage startups. A subsequent step may involve partnering with a startup studio to invest in and support a small number of ventures, with the option to acquire some of them down the way. The next step is to establish venture builders to develop strategic initiatives internally, a model suitable only for firms with significant budgets and more mature Open Innovation capabilities. Finally, firms with greater experience in Open Innovation have evolved their intrapreneurship programs into open platforms by integrating external startups, thereby consolidating all early-stage deal flow through a unified structure. In this setup, Venture Builders can scale the most promising initiatives emerging from both internal and external sources.
- Horizon 3: In today's environment, characterized by rapid technological change and cross-industry adoption, identifying future trends and areas for diversification has become increasingly challenging for companies, regardless of size or sector. To anticipate emerging opportunities, firms must connect closely with innovative startups and ecosystems. However, startups are often reluctant to engage with corporates lacking a clear business or strategic agenda. As a first step, companies at the early stage of their Open Innovation journey should consider establishing an Innovation Antenna in one of the main tech ecosystems to identify future innovation trends and expose R&D and business units to emerging technologies and business models. As firms mature their Open Innovation experience, they may scale their international presence by setting up multiple antennas across additional tech hubs. Popular destinations among global innovation leaders include Israel, Seoul, Dubai and the US East Coast, alongside European centers of excellence such as London, Paris, Berlin and Barcelona (Mind the Bridge, 2016). Ultimately, companies may deepen their engagement within targeted global innovation hubs by establishing a Corporate Innovation Outpost (a more structured local presence designed to support international scouting activities and upskill innovation teams). Another strategic pathway to gain exposure to disruptive technologies and emerging business models is through startup investments. As seen, large corporates often set up a dedicated CVC fund to build a portfolio of startups and scaleups to be closely monitored. For companies in earlier stages of their Open Innovation journey, a less resource-intensive alternative involves participating as Limited Partners in third-party venture funds or conducting off-balance sheet investments. These approaches allow firms to gain experience with startup investment processes without committing the substantial capital required for a full-scale CVC structure.

As discussed, Open Innovation initiatives and models are continuously evolving; new models emerge, while others consolidate or, in some cases, decline. An emerging trend in the Open Innovation field is the growing hybridization of Open Innovation tools, as corporates experiment with blended approaches to bridge different innovation horizons and engage startups at varying stages of maturity (Fig. 3.7). As anticipated, intrapreneurship programs, frequently led by innovation units rather than HR, are increasingly incorporating contributions from external startups, effectively becoming one-stop shops for early-stage ideas and, in some cases, replacing Corporate Accelerators. At the same time, though still in their infancy, new approaches like Corporate Venture Builders and Startup Studios are gaining traction reflecting the heterogeneity of current solutions. Open Innovation Outposts in leading tech hubs (e.g., Silicon Valley, Israel, the US East Coast, South Korea) are expanding, most often in the leaner form of Antennas, frequently operated in collaboration with third-party providers deeply embedded in the local ecosystem (Mind the Bridge, 2024d). Other models are moving into a stage of consolidation. The Venture Client model has become a "must-have", with a recent trend toward its productization: innovation and matching platforms, with some integrating startup relationship management features, are proliferating, while startup scouting is increasingly shifting toward AI-driven tools. In addition, new tools such as "Validation Sprints"[4] are being developed to assess the feasibility and viability of projects originating out from intrapreneurship programs, selectively funneling the most promising initiatives into Venture Builder for further development and scaling. CVC continues to show momentum, although many corporates quietly scale back or discontinue investments, while others spin off their CVC arms into independent, VC-like funds[5] (Mind the Bridge, 2023a).

In theory, the dynamics of corporate-startup collaboration are understood, but in practice, successful management remains a significant puzzle whose solution lies in case-study examination.

[4] A validation sprint is a series of experiments designed to test and either confirm or reject assumptions about a business idea, a product or a service.

[5] Some reference case are Siemens (Next47), Allianz (AV8 Ventures), E.ON (Future Energy Ventures), Deutsche Telekom (DTCP), BBVA (Propel Ventures), Santander (Mouro Capital) and SAP (Sapphire).

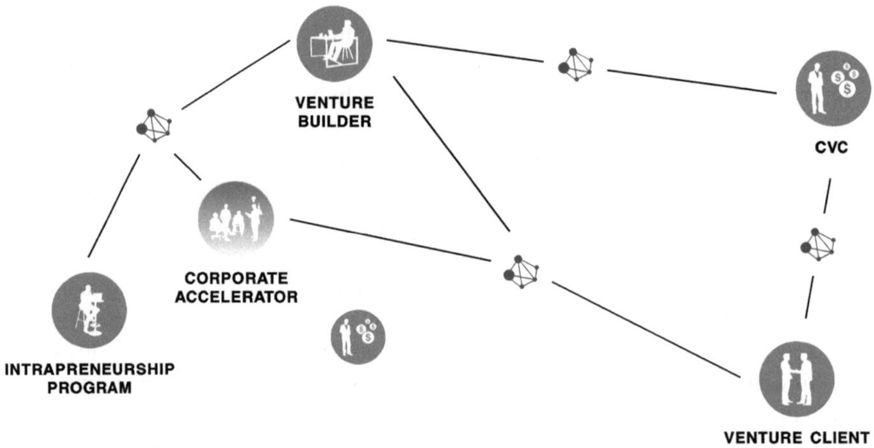

Fig. 3.7 The hybridization of Open Innovation models. *Source* Own elaboration adapted from Mind the Bridge (2023a)

References

Amo, B. W. (2010). Corporate entrepreneurship and intrapreneurship related to innovation behaviour among employees. *International Journal of Entrepreneurial Venturing, 2*(2), 144–158. https://doi.org/10.1504/IJEV.2010.034819

Antoncic, B., & Hisrich, R. D. (2001). Intrapreneurship: Construct refinement and cross-cultural validation. *Journal of Business Venturing, 16*(5), 495–527. https://doi.org/10.1016/S0883-9026(99)00054-3

Baghai, M., Coley, S., & White, D. (1999). *The alchemy of growth: Practical insights for building the enduring enterprise*. Perseus Books.

Baumann, O., Bergenholtz, C., Frederiksen, L., Grant, R. M., Köhler, R., Preston, D. L., & Shane, S. (2018). Rocket internet: Organizing a startup factory. *Journal of Organization Design, 7*(1), 1–15. https://doi.org/10.1186/s41469-018-0037-2

Belingheri, P., & Lechner, C. (2025). *Venture builders and the creation of scaleups: De-risking entrepreneurship to drive high-growth companies*. Springer Nature Switzerland.

Bosma, N., Wennekers, S., Guerrero, M., Amor'os, J. E., Martiarena, A., & Singer, S. (2013). Global entrepreneurship monitor, special report on entrepreneurship employee activity. https://www.gemconsortium.org/file/open?fileId=48592

Boyacıoğlu, B., Özdemir, M. N., & Karim, S. (2024). Acqui-hires: Redeployment and retention of human capital post-acquisition. *Strategic Management Journal, 45*(2), 205–237. https://doi.org/10.1002/smj.3556

Brouthers, K. D., Chen, L., Li, S., & Shaheer, N. (2022). Charting new courses to enter foreign markets: Conceptualization, theoretical framework, and research directions on non-traditional entry modes. *Journal of International Business Studies, 53*(9), 2088. https://doi.org/10.1057/s41267-022-00521-x

Brueller, N. N., & Capron, L. (2021). Acquisitions of startups by incumbents: The 3 cs of co-specialization from startup inception to post-merger integration. *California Management Review, 63*(3), 70–93. https://doi.org/10.1177/0008125621996502

Burgers, J. H., & Covin, J. G. (2016). The contingent effects of differentiation and integration on corporate entrepreneurship. *Strategic Management Journal, 37*(3), 521–540. https://doi.org/10.1002/smj.2343

Chesbrough, H. (2003). *Open innovation: The new imperative for creating and profiting from technology*. Harvard Business Press.

Chesbrough, H. (2006). *Open business models: How to thrive in the new innovation landscape*. Harvard Business Press.

Chesbrough, H. (2024). A reconsideration of open innovation after 20 years. In H. Chesbrough, A. Radziwon, W. Vanhaverbeke, & J. West (Eds.), *The Oxford handbook of open innovation* (pp. 3–18). Oxford University Press.

Chesbrough, H., & Bogers, M. (2014). Explicating open innovation: Clarifying an emerging paradigm for understanding innovation. In H. Chesbrough, W. Vanhaverbeke, & J. West (Eds.), *New frontiers in open innovation* (pp. 3–28). Oxford University Press.

Chesbrough, H., & Tucci, C. L. (2004). Corporate venture capital in the context of corporate innovation. *Conference proceedings of the DRUID summer conference* (pp. 14-16).

Chesbrough, H. W. (2002). Making sense of corporate venture capital. *Harvard Business Review, 80*(3), 90–99.

Chiaroni, D., Chiesa, V., & Frattini, F. (2010). Unravelling the process from closed to open innovation: Evidence from mature, asset-intensive industries. *R&D Management, 40*(3), 222–245. https://doi.org/10.1111/j.1467-9310.2010.00589.x

Chiaroni, D., Chiesa, V., & Frattini, F. (2011). The open innovation journey: How firms dynamically implement the emerging innovation management paradigm. *Technovation, 31*(1), 34–43. https://doi.org/10.1016/j.technovation.2009.08.007

Cohen, S., Fehder, D. C., Hochberg, Y. V., & Murray, F. (2019). The design of startup accelerators. *Research Policy, 48*(7), 1781–1797. https://doi.org/10.1016/j.respol.2019.04.003

Cunningham, C., Ederer, F., & Ma, S. (2021). Killer acquisitions. *Journal of Political Economy, 129*(3), 649–702. https://doi.org/10.1086/712506

Curry, A., & Hodgson, A. (2008). Seeing in multiple horizons: Connecting futures to vision and strategy. In R. Slaughter & A. Hines (Eds.), *The knowledge base of futures studies* (pp. 66–85). APF.

Decreton, B., Monteiro, F., Frangos, J. M., & Friedman, L. (2021). Innovation outposts in entrepreneurial ecosystems: How to make them more successful. *California Management Review, 63*(3), 94–117. https://doi.org/10.1177/0008125621996494

Drucker, P. F. (1986). *Innovation and entrepreneurship: Practice and principles*. Simon and Schuster.

Dushnitsky, G., & Lenox, M. J. (2005). When do firms undertake R&D by investing in new ventures? *Strategic Management Journal, 26*(10), 947–965. https://doi.org/10.1002/smj.488

Dushnitsky, G., & Lenox, M. J. (2006). When does corporate venture capital investment create firm value? *Journal of Business Venturing, 21*(6), 753–772. https://doi.org/10.1016/j.jbusvent.2005.04.012

Enkel, E., Bell, J., & Hogenkamp, H. (2011). Open innovation maturity framework. *International Journal of Innovation Management, 15*(06), 1161–1189. https://doi.org/10.1142/S1363919611003696

Enkel, E., Gassmann, O., & Chesbrough, H. (2009). Open R&D and open innovation: Exploring the phenomenon. *R&D Management, 39*(4), 311–316. https://doi.org/10.1111/j.1467-9310.2009.00570.x

Gassmann, O., & Enkel, E. (2004). Towards a theory of open innovation: three core process archetypes. *Conference Proceedings of the R&D Management Conference (RADMA)*, 2004.

Gassmann, O., Enkel, E., & Chesbrough, H. (2010). The future of open innovation. *R&D Management, 40*(3), 213–221. https://doi.org/10.1111/j.1467-9310.2010.00605.x

Gimmy, G., Kanbach, D., Stubner, S., Konig, A., & Enders, A. (2017, July 27). What BMW'S corporate VC offers that regular investors can't. *Harvard Business Review*. https://hbr.org/2017/07/what-bmws-corporate-vc-offers-that-regular-investors-cant

Gutmann, T. (2019). Harmonizing corporate venturing modes: An integrative review and research agenda. *Management Review Quarterly, 69*(2), 121–157. https://doi.org/10.1007/s11301-018-0148-4

Gutmann, T., Chochoiek, C., & Chesbrough, H. (2023). Extending open innovation: Orchestrating knowledge flows from corporate venture capital investments. *California Management Review, 65*(2), 45–70. https://doi.org/10.1177/00081256221 1473

Gutmann, T., & Lang, C. (2022). Unlocking the magic of corporate-startup collaboration: How to make it work. *IEEE Engineering Management Review, 50*(2), 19–25. https://doi.org/10.1109/EMR.2022.3158490

Hernández-Perlines, F., Ariza-Montes, A., & Blanco-González-Tejero, C. (2022). Intrapreneurship research: A comprehensive literature review. *Journal of Business Research, 153*, 428–444. https://doi.org/10.1016/j.jbusres.2022.08.015

Kim, J. D. (2022). Startup acquisitions, relocation, and employee entrepreneurship. *Strategic Management Journal, 43*(11), 2189–2216. https://doi.org/10.1002/smj.3408

Kohler, T. (2016). Corporate accelerators: Building bridges between corporations and startups. *Business Horizons, 59*(3), 347–357. https://doi.org/10.1016/j.bushor.2016.01.008

March, J. G. (1991). Exploration and exploitation in organizational learning. *Organization Science, 2*(1), 71–87. https://doi.org/10.1287/orsc.2.1.71

McGrath, R. G., Keil, T., & Tukiainen, T. (2006). Extracting value from corporate venturing. *MIT Sloan Management Review, 48*(1), 50–56.

Mind the Bridge. (2016). EU corporate innovation outposts in Silicon Valley. The Who's Who. https://mindthebridge.com/eu-corporate-outposts-silicon-valley-whos-v-1-report-2016/

Mind the Bridge. (2022). Evolve or be extinct—Open innovation models for the future. https://mindthebridge.com/evolve-or-be-extinct/

Mind the Bridge. (2023a). Open innovation: The age of hybridization and results—Evolve or be extinct. https://mindthebridge.com/2023-open-innovation-evolve-or-be-extinct/.

Mind the Bridge. (2023b). Corporate innovation outposts in Silicon Valley | 2023 report update. https://mindthebridge.com/2023-outposts-corporate-silicon-valley/.

Mind the Bridge. (2023c). Corporate innovation in South Korea. https://mindthebridge.com/corporate-innovation-in-south-korea-report-2023/

Mind the Bridge. (2023d). Corporate innovation outposts in Israel. https://mindthebridge.com/2023-outposts-corporate-israel/

Mind the Bridge. (2024). *2024c*. Innovation or Isolation. https://mindthebridge.com/innovation-or-isolation-the-future-of-regional-ecosystems-startup-ecosystem-stars-report-2024/

Mind the Bridge. (2024a). The open innovation imperative: adapting to stay competitive-evolve or be extinct season 2024. https://mindthebridge.com/the-open-innovation-imperative-adapting-to-stay-competitive-evolve-or-be-extinct-season-2024/

Mind the Bridge. (2024b). Benchmarking Venture Client. A Global Comparison | 2024 Report. https://mindthebridge.com/2024-open-innovation-venture-client/

Mind the Bridge. (2024d). Japanese corporate innovation outposts in the US East Coast. https://mindthebridge.com/2024-outposts-japanese-us-east-coast/

Mind the Bridge. (2024e). The end of the Startup M&a era? Tech Startup M&a 2024 report. https://mindthebridge.com/the-end-of-the-startup-ma-era-tech-startup-ma-2024-report/

Mind the Bridge. (2025a). Benchmarking intrapreneurship - a global comparison. Forthcoming: https://mindthebridge.com/research/

Mind the Bridge. (2025b). CVC investments. Data and Models. Forthcoming: https://mindthebridge.com/research/

Mind the Bridge. (2025c). Open Innovation Outlook 2025. Trends in Corporate–Startup Engagement. https://mindthebridge.com/open-innovation-outlook-2025-trends-for-2025-in-corporate-startup-engagement/

Mind the Bridge and ICC. (2022). Gold standards for the world's companies to incorporate open innovation and corporate-startup collaboration– Best practices for worldwide companies and SMEs emerging from corporate startup stars awards. https://mindthebridge.com/2022-open-innovation-gold-standards/

Neessen, P. C., Caniëls, M. C., Vos, B., & De Jong, J. P. (2019). The intrapreneurial employee: Toward an integrated model of intrapreneurship and research agenda. *International*

Entrepreneurship and Management Journal, 15(2), 545–571. https://doi.org/10.1007/s11365-018-0552-1
Nesta. (2015). Winning Together—a guide to successful corporate-startup collaborations. https://media.nesta.org.uk/documents/winning-_together-june-2015.pdf
O'Reilly, C. A., & Tushman, M. L. (2004). The ambidextrous organization. *Harvard Business Review, 82*(4), 74–83.
Onetti, A. (2021a). Turning open innovation into practice: Trends in European corporates. *Journal of Business Strategy, 42*(1), 51–58. https://doi.org/10.1108/JBS-07-2019-0138
Onetti, A. (2021b, August). *24.* Four questions to ask when setting up a venture builder: https://sifted.eu/articles/venture-builder-characteristics
Onetti, A. (2021c). *April 13.* Sorry not everything is a venture builder. https://sifted.eu/articles/venture-builders-type
Onetti, A. (2021d, November 16). The venture builder as a bridge: The BP Launchapd model. *Sifted.* https://sifted.eu/articles/venture-builder-cvc-bp-launchpad
Parker, S. C. (2011). Intrapreneurship or entrepreneurship? *Journal of Business Venturing, 26*(1), 19–34. https://doi.org/10.1016/j.jbusvent.2009.07.003
Pinchot, G. (1985). *Intrapreneuring.* Harper & Row.
Pisoni, A., & Onetti, A. (2018). When startups exit: Comparing strategies in Europe and the USA. *Journal of Business Strategy, 39*(3), 26–33. https://doi.org/10.1108/JBS-02-2017-0022
Qin, F., Wright, M., & Gao, J. (2019). Accelerators and intra-ecosystem variety: How entrepreneurial agency influences venture development in a time-compressed support program. *Industrial and Corporate Change, 28*(4), 961–975. https://doi.org/10.1093/icc/dtz036
Roschek, B., & Jones, E. (2024). Open R&D in large corporations. In H. Chesbrough, A. Radziwon, W. Vanhaverbeke, & J. West (Eds.), *The Oxford handbook of open innovation* (pp. 715–728). Oxford University Press.
Sauvage, N., Zeisberger, C., & Varadan, M. (2022, July 28). Is corporate venture capital right for your startup? *Harvard Business Review.*. https://hbr.org/2022/07/is-corporate-venture-capital-right-for-your-startup
Seitz, N., Lehmann, E. E., & Haslanger, P. (2024). Corporate accelerators: Design and startup performance. *Small Business Economics, 62*(4), 1615–1640.
Sinha, N., & Srivastava, K. B. (2013). Association of personality, work values and socio-cultural factors with intrapreneurial orientation. *The Journal of Entrepreneurship, 22*(1), 97–113. https://doi.org/10.1177/0971355712469186
Siota, J., Alunni, A., Riveros-ChacÃn, P., Wilson, M., & Karlsson Dinnetz, M. (2020). *Corporate venturing: Insights for European leaders in government, university and industry*, EUR 30060 EN. *Publications Office of the European Union, Luxembourg.* https://doi.org/10.2760/976372
Stenholm, D., Moore, D., Leifer, L., & Bergsjö, D. (2018). Fail early, fail often: Exploring Stanford's ME310 course as a basis to improve innovation outpost efficacy. In DS 92: *Proceedings of the DESIGN 2018 15th international design conference* (pp. 2505-2516). https://doi.org/10.21278/idc.2018.0503
Strebulaev, I. A., & Wang, A. (2021). *Organizational Structure and Decision-Making in Corporate Venture Capital.* https://doi.org/10.2139/ssrn.3963514
Urbano, D., Turro, A., Wright, M., & Zahra, S. (2022). Corporate entrepreneurship: A systematic literature review and future research agenda. *Small Business Economics, 59*(4), 1541–1565. https://doi.org/10.1007/s11187-021-00590-6
Weiblen, T., & Chesbrough, H. W. (2015). Engaging with startups to enhance corporate innovation. *California Management Review, 57*(2), 66–90. https://doi.org/10.1525/cmr.2015.57.2.66
Zahra, S. A. (1991). Predictors and financial outcomes of corporate entrepreneurship: An exploratory study. *Journal of Business Venturing, 6*(4), 259–285. https://doi.org/10.1016/0883-9026(91)90019-A

Chapter 4
Open Innovation Deconstructed

Abstract The best way to understand Open Innovation is to look at how top-performing companies actually apply it and, even more importantly, how their approaches have evolved and continue to evolve. This chapter analyzes 15 case studies that showcase the concrete implementation of Open Innovation and the emerging models of corporate-startup collaboration. Particular attention is given to the most recent trend toward hybrid approaches. We explore the models and modes adopted, the strategic objectives pursued, as well as the challenges encountered along the way.

Keywords Corporate-startup collaboration · OI implementation · Strategic objectives · Challenges

4.1 Use-Cases of Corporate-Startup Collaboration

The following case studies of corporate-startup collaborations are drawn from innovation leaders recognized in the most recent Corporate Startup Stars Awards (Mind the Bridge, 2024).

Emerging evidence highlights a clear trend: Open Innovation is not a fixed formula, but rather a dynamic process that evolves in response to shifting technologies, markets, and societal demands (Mind the Bridge, 2025). The growing transition toward more hybrid, inclusive, and strategically embedded approaches underscores its role as a critical driver of sustainable growth and long-term competitive advantage.

These use-cases may serve as inspiration for organizations willing to embrace this evolution, internalize the lessons learned, and adopt multifaceted strategies that position them to lead future innovation and industry transformation.

Thanks to exclusive access to Mind the Bridge's expertise in connecting startups and corporates to maximize growth potential, the most compelling case studies are presented in the following pages. Each provides insights into diverse Open Innovation initiatives—ranging from Intrapreneurship, Accelerators, Venture Builders, and Venture Clients to CVC and M&A—as introduced in the previous chapter. They also

A. Onetti and A. Pisoni, *Open Innovation in Action*,
SpringerBriefs in Entrepreneurship and Innovation,
https://doi.org/10.1007/978-3-032-17332-4_4

shed light on key organizational perspectives, including strategy, structure, culture, and processes.

4.2 Case Studies

4.2.1 3 M—From Strategic CVC to Business Building: New Growth Ventures

Established in 2008, 3 M Ventures has been a pioneering player in the Corporate Venture Capital (CVC) arena. In 2023, New Growth Ventures was formed which combines 3 M's CVC with a cross-functional Business Building team. New Growth Ventures (NGV) is under the leadership of Mark Copman and aims to accelerate the development of innovative business opportunities.

3 M Ventures, the CVC arm, continues to invest in startups that align with the company's strategic growth priorities. The Business Building team focuses on internal growth initiatives, targeting Horizon 2 and 3 opportunities. These two teams—the investment team and the Business Building team—work seamlessly together, with a strong emphasis on partnering with and investing in startups.

3 M Ventures operates as a strategic CVC arm, investing globally. 3 M Ventures works in close alignment with company business groups (BGs). The process begins by identifying strategic growth objectives and pinpointing gaps in internal programs that could be addressed through external technologies or innovative business models. Potential startups are assessed by a dedicated committee, which then appoints a champion to lead the collaboration between 3 M and the startup.

The champion facilitates collaborations with the startup to accelerate commercialization. An example is the collaboration with Gray Matter Robotics, that resulted in the development of a co-marketing agreement in the abrasives automation sector. The New Growth Ventures Business Building team currently has 12 active programs. On average, 2–3 programs per year reach the validation stage and 1–2 the commercialization stage. Programs are supported by the R&D annual budget. Any revenue is reinvested to help these businesses grow. When programs reach critical mass, they are either integrated into an existing business unit or spun out if no clear path to a business unit exists.

A recent example is NGV's automated manufacturing collaboration with EVOLOH to support their vision for low-cost renewable hydrogen production. Another key collaboration is a joint development agreement (JDA) with Svante, a company specializing in point source carbon capture technologies. This partnership focuses on leveraging parallel channel structured adsorbent technology to create scalable solutions for the Carbon Dioxide Removal industry.

4.2.2 ACCIONA—From Venture Client to Strategic Acquisition

The I'MNOVATION initiative by ACCIONA, launched in 2016, is an Open Innovation program that collaborates with startups, scaleups, spin-offs, universities, and R&D centers to co-develop sustainable technological solutions.

The program targets challenges in areas such as climate change, water scarcity, and resilient infrastructure. When selected for I'MNOVATION initiative, companies receive financial support with co-development costs covered by ACCIONA along with expert mentorship, and technical guidance. Each selected project receives a budget of €50 k for development. ACCIONA provides a dedicated team of mentors, workspace for pilot development, and networking opportunities with other program participants.

This helps startups develop and bring their solutions to market by leveraging ACCIONA's resources and expertise. Through 55 innovation challenges thus far, the program has analyzed over 1,000 startups, filtered 120 and run 60 pilots. As of now, the program continues to support innovative projects, with 16 ongoing challenges from energy efficiency and renewable asset monitoring to irrigation optimization.

The most interesting angle is the strategic opportunities for ACCIONA triggered by startups. In 2021, ACCIONA acquired Silence, a Spanish electric scooter startup, positioning itself as a leader in Europe's electric mobility market by 2024. This acquisition also paved the way for the launch of Acciona's new business line, featuring the S04 electric urban NanoCar with removable batteries, produced by Silence. SAALG Geomechanics, a software and engineering startup from Spain, has developed technology to predict ground movements during construction. It was part of the 6th edition of I'MNOVATION run in 2023 and later on raised €3.65 million in funding with Acciona as the lead investor.

4.2.3 Bosch B/S/H—How Venture Client Can Boost Adoption

BSH Startup Kitchen, the dedicated Venture Client unit of BSH Home Appliances Group, was established in late 2018 to bring innovative startup solutions into the company. Around the same time, similar Venture Client activities were launched at the broader Bosch Group level under the Open Bosch network. Given the very different nature of business and organizational setup, BSH Startup Kitchen embarked on its own journey to deploy Venture Client. Nevertheless, both BSH Startup Kitchen and Open Bosch have since developed a well-connected relationship, allowing them to leverage synergies where beneficial, while retaining operational independence.

In its early stages, BSH Startup Kitchen succeeded fast in identifying critical challenges of the company to address, but it initially struggled to secure the long-term adoption of new solutions. Through several initial projects and fast iteration of learnings and adopting its operations, the team discovered that success lay not in rushing through implementations, but in focusing on quality and ensuring compliance with relevant company standards throughout the process. Based on this principle, BSH Startup Kitchen built a strong network not only to business teams, but also with essential stakeholders across IT, Purchasing, Legal, and other areas which have become supporters and promoters of Open Innovation activities. This allowed the team to refine its processes, streamline operations, and involve key experts and decision-makers from the outset. Not only does BSH Startup Kitchen identify and validate startup solutions, but it also actively supports business teams in the long-term adoption of these solutions, ensuring that innovative ideas are fully integrated and sustained within BSH. Eventually, BSH Startup Kitchen views itself as an integral part of BSH's strategic initiatives, supporting the company's goals rather than acting as a standalone innovation unit.

Since its founding, BSH Startup Kitchen has completed over 140 projects, achieving an adoption rate of more than 40%, delivering solid and measurable business impact along the full value chain of BSH Home Appliances Group. Successful collaborations of the past years include the introduction of an external microplastic filter solution for BSH washing machines, developed together with the UK-startup Matter/Inheriting Earth. This innovation, presented to the market by BSH in September 2024, supports the company's commitment to improving the quality of life for its consumers and enhancing sustainability. Another noteworthy collaboration is the onboarding and company-wide rollout of Synthesia, a synthetic video creation tool that has revolutionized how BSH creates and uses video content for both internal and external purposes.

4.2.4 EDF—From Intrapreneurship to New Business Creation

EDF Pulse Incubation is EDF Group's internal Venture Building program, designed to transform innovative ideas into new businesses. Operating since 2017, the program enables intrapreneurs by providing financial resources, expertise, and a structured path to develop and scale new ventures. Its mission extends beyond revenue generation, adding strategic value to long-term priorities in energy transition and decarbonation.

Projects pass selection gates based on the strategic value and fit as well as scalability (targeting €500 M+ markets). Proposals must also demonstrate realistic commercialization potential within 24 months and ability to secure support from EDF Group. The first stage (START) is about validating the initial concept and forming a cohesive team. Once the solution is aligned with market needs and internal capabilities (MATCH), prototype development and market testing are conducted to validate its feasibility (TEST). Finally, projects with proven commercial traction and a validated business model are launched as independent subsidiaries (LAUNCH). Since its inception, EDF Pulse Incubation has successfully launched twelve subsidiaries.

These ventures now collectively employ nearly 300 people and generate combined annual revenues exceeding €15 M. Startups begin as wholly owned subsidiaries under EDF Pulse Holdings. They may later come back to the core business units if they are operating a business model deeply connected to theirs. Or they may open up to external investors to support further growth. As these ventures mature, EDF may cede majority ownership for some of them, allowing them to scale independently. The shareholding structure remains adaptable, with decisions made case by case based on what best serves each venture's growth trajectory and the EDF Group's strategic interests. A recent example is OKLIMA, a subsidiary of EDF Group that emerged from the EDF Pulse Incubation program in 2023. Specializing in carbon contribution, OKLIMA develops projects that contribute to carbon sequestration through natural based solutions. Another case is METROSCOPE, a subsidiary offering SaaS solutions for industrial diagnostics. Launched in 2018, it has grown into a global business serving high-profile clients and expanding its operations across multiple countries.

4.2.5 W-PIT Japan Airlines—Intrapreneurship to Develop Purpose-Driven Ventures

W-PIT (Wakuwaku-Platform Innovation Team) is an internal initiative launched by Japan Airlines (JAL) in March 2017 by Shiro Matsuzaki. Its objective is to support the company's evolution from a traditional, legacy organization into a more innovative entity.

W-PIT originated from JAL's "IT Innovation Lab", an internal project designed to foster digital transformation and collaboration across departments. Employees voluntarily participated in hackathon-style events. One of the participating teams focused on "Wakuwaku"—a concept representing excitement and individual passion—and evolved into W-PIT. Initially starting with two members, W-PIT has expanded to involve 220 members by 2024. W-PIT operates as an independent unit within JAL, with members balancing their primary roles while participating in W-PIT activities.

Following a Semi-Annual Program Model, W-PIT recruits new projects every six months through an internal application process, receiving around 100 ideas per year. Employees dedicate 20% of their time to the program, which follows a five-stage selection process (Stage&Gate): Idea Submission, Selection, Project Launch, Pitch, and Commercialization.

W-PIT has launched several projects that explore new business opportunities while also aiming to generate positive social impact. One of its standout ventures, "JAL Sauna Travel" package offers customizable sauna-themed travel, allowing customers to combine flights and local sauna experiences. The travel package creates personalized itineraries, showcasing lesser-known local attractions. Since its launch, JAL Sauna Travel, has achieved $2 million in ARR. Other successful projects include the "Blue Sky Study Abroad Program" (2021) which enhances educational access by connecting students with global learning opportunities and fostering cultural exchange.

For Japan Airlines, this program not only strengthens its community engagement by supporting local producers and regions across Japan, but contributes to regional revitalization. Additionally, the "Co-creation Project with Heralbony" (2021) showcased artwork created by individuals with disabilities, promoting social inclusion and raising awareness through art.

W-PIT has significantly contributed to reshape JAL's internal culture by encouraging cross-functional collaboration and enabling employees to engage in projects beyond their regular duties. Looking forward, W-PIT aims to transform its co-creation activities into a business platform that extends beyond the airline industry to also engage external partners from various sectors.

4.2.6 Maersk—Driving Innovation through Venture Investments and Strategic Venture Client

In the summer of 2023, Maersk Growth sharpened its focus on supporting A.P. Moller-Maersk's sustainability ambitions and pivoted to concentrate all future investments on the Energy Transition while continuing to engage with the Supply Chain Tech ecosystem through Venture Clienting. This new mandate underscores Maersk Growth's role as a driving force in A. P. Moller—Maersk's green and digital transformation in maritime logistics.

Operating at the intersection of corporate strategy and startup collaboration, Maersk Growth has developed a streamlined, business-led Venture Client process. This approach fosters mutual value creation as partnering with startups at various stages of maturity, allows Maersk and startups to implement new technologies in collaboration. Whether collaborating on pilot projects or developing proofs of concept, this model enables Maersk to identify and adopt new solutions, while offering startups strategic guidance, the opportunity to test at scale, and potentially onboard Maersk as a customer.

In parallel, the Venture Capital arm Maersk Growth focuses on securing investments in startups pioneering energy transition and low-carbon technologies, helping future-proof Maersk's operations and supporting the company's role in the global energy transition. Through both investments and partnerships, Maersk Growth is advancing technologies essential for net zero emissions and operational efficiency. An example of this collaborative model in action is Maersk's partnership with Pactum, an AI-powered platform for supplier contract negotiations, resulting in faster procurement processes. In 2024, Maersk also supported Pactum's Series B funding round, reinforcing the long-term value of such strategic partnerships.

The strategic shift in Maersk Growth underlines the company's understanding of corporate-startup collaboration. By integrating both Venture Capital and Venture Client approaches, Maersk Growth strengthens Maersk's position in sustainable logistics and enables startups to address challenges across supply chain tech and energy transition.

4.2.7 Olam—Externalizing Venture Building

In 2018, OLAM International, a Singapore-based agri-business company, embarked on OLAM's Engine 2.0 initiative to accelerate their industry's digitalization. In 2022, as part of its strategic plan, OLAM externalized its innovation unit by establishing Nupo Ventures, a wholly owned independent Venture Studio aimed at accelerating digital-first solutions in agriculture and food (key areas: future-ready supply chains, regenerating food systems, and sustainable consumers).

The newly developed ventures are fully owned by Nupo Ventures but modeled as external startups. During the ideation phase, an assigned team collaborates with internal and external market experts to clearly define problems and solutions. This process generally lasts for 6 months. Once the idea is validated, the next step involves developing a Minimum Viable Product (MVP).

Since its launch, Nupo Ventures built 6 ventures out of 7 exploratory topics. As of today, two ventures, Terrascope and JIVA, are still active, while in 2023 they launched a new venture called TRACT in collaboration with over 30 companies. JIVA—a digital platform for farmer services—has broadened its offering and attracted new clients, achieving a 58% increase in revenue in 2023. In 2024, JIVA launched a private label, further enhancing its market presence. Recognized by the UN at the SDG Digital Acceleration Conference, JIVA focuses on uplifting smallholder farming communities by engaging with over 100,000 farmers. Moreover, 25% of 500 farmers interviewed in 2023 reported an increase in income, and 90% perceived a positive impact in their communities. This success has positively impacted Nupo Venture in 2023, which recorded double-digit growth in both sales and revenues—32% and 57.9%, respectively—laying the foundation to power their business in the years to come.

Despite being in its early development stage, JIVA was recently honored by Stewardship Asia Centre (SAC) as one of the SL25 winners displaying steward leadership. Similarly, Terrascope has been recognized as a 2024 Indo Pacific Climate Tech 100 Company, by Indo Pacific Economic Framework for Prosperity (IPEF). OLAM envisions Nupo Ventures to become fully independent, with the ventures capable of raising external funds.

4.2.8 Repsol—Combining Open Innovation Tools

Repsol's approach is built on a comprehensive Open Innovation strategy, initiated in 2016 with the launch of the CVC arm and expanded in 2020 with the formation of a dedicated Open Innovation team. At the heart of this strategy is IdeaAction, created in

2021, Repsol's Venture Clienting initiative that sources innovative technology from universities, R&D centers, and startups.

Since 2021, over 40 PoCs have been launched under this initiative, with projects receiving a €50,000 budget and a 3–6 month timeline for implementation. More than 50% have moved to further development within Repsol's business units. Repsol Technology Lab with 230 scientists serves as testing ground, ensuring each PoC undergoes industrial validation and refinement. An example is Finboot Tech, where Repsol validated a blockchain-based tool to trace renewable fuel use, ensuring CO_2 reductions. The tool has been piloted on two buses in Madrid, with plans to expand and explore new use-cases.

Alongside IdeaAction, Repsol Entrepreneurs Fund serves as Repsol's corporate Accelerator, supporting early-stage startups through convertible loans, real-world testing, and tailored mentoring. Since its inception, it has backed 77 startups, completing over 950 pilot tests, raising more than €450 million, and achieving a 70% survival rate among its participants.

Repsol's Corporate Venturing is the strategic investment vehicle targeting new business models and disruptive technologies. Established in 2016, Repsol Deep Tech Fund, entered its second cycle in 2022 with €50 million allocated for early-stage investments, from seed to Series A. This initiative has driven nearly €130 million in investments across 30+ companies, with a current portfolio of 21 startups aligned with Repsol's innovation goals. A standout investment includes Smarkia, an energy optimization SaaS platform. Repsol acquired a 33% stake and commercialized one of its proprietary optimization technologies. Repsol also actively cultivates partnerships that drive innovation, such as SC Net Zero Ventures (NZV), launched in 2023 in partnership with Suma Capital to support later-stage investments in energy transition technologies and accelerate large-scale deployments. Approved by Spain's CNMV (National Securities Market Commission), NZV had its first close at €125 million in 2024.

Additionally, in 2023, Repsol introduced All4Zero, an industrial innovation hub in collaboration with ArcelorMittal, Holcim España, and Iberia, aimed at identifying, testing, and scaling decarbonization technologies. From 186 proposals, 12 projects were selected to develop proofs of concept, showcasing Repsol's commitment to sustainable industrial practices and innovation through collaboration.

4.2.9 Siemens—The Bridge from Intrapreneurship to Venture Building

Siemens has embraced the need to be ambidextrous, striking a balance between exploiting its established business lines and cultivating new, exploratory business-building capabilities.

To power this "exploit and explore" approach, Siemens has built internal Innovation Accelerators, programs and platforms that empower people to connect

Intrapreneurship with Venture Building within a corporate setting. The focus is on delivering value to the customer, while maintaining a strong business perspective—just like startups. The Siemens Innovation Ecosystem connects more than 120,000 colleagues across businesses and regions in over 100 innovation funnels and co-ideation campaigns per year. This platform collects ideas around future products and services, accompanying intrapreneurs from ideation to launch. Thereby it builds the bridge between Siemens' strategic future markets and the businesses innovation. The Validation Engine "ChatGPT & Co Ideation Challenge" is an example where the use-cases submitted laid the foundation for a company-wide AI radar.

The Intrapreneurs Bootcamp is a program to empower serial intrapreneurs and thus increase the innovation capacity of the company. Since its start in 2016, more than 400 intrapreneurs from 35 countries and across Siemens have tested 92 business ideas with 2000+ customer interviews in 14 cohorts. The program has a lasting impact on the participants: Intrapreneurs create ripples across their organization with "one intrapreneur impacting 11 others" showing significantly stronger customer focus and collaboration across hierarchies and functions in their daily job.

The Validation Engine, hosted by Siemens' Factory Automation Business to ensure close collaboration and exchange with innovation teams, is an Accelerator program that drives business model validation through direct customer engagement. This initiative is available to all Siemens employees. It uses an evidence-based, customer-centric approach that enables fast validation focused on market-driven innovation. The Validation Engine aims to minimize risk by 'validating' new ventures against real customer needs and market demand before further investment. The first phase of the program focuses on understanding customer pain points and challenges, while the second involves promising ventures participating in paid pilots. Since its inception, more than 60 innovation projects over the past 3 years have gone through the Validation Engine, with over 4,000 customer interviews conducted to gather feedback. The program has involved more than 350 Siemens employees. Importantly, the Validation Engine has also helped Siemens avoid investing in ventures lacking market potential, with 80% of the projects being "invalidated" based on customer feedback.

One example from the Validation Engine is Virtual Continuous Web (VCW), an internal corporate startup focused on improving battery cell production processes. After entering the Validation Engine, the VCW team conducted more than 100 interviews with various functions in both startup and incumbent companies, including Process Engineering, Quality Management/Assurance, and Production Planning. VCW engaged in a paid pilot project with a pre-selected customer. Having successfully passed the Validation Engine, the team is now in the incubation phase, which means setting up their idea for scaling and getting customer traction.

4.2.10 *Sodexo—Driving Sustainability Innovation through Collaboration and Intrapreneurship*

Since its launch in 2016, Innov'Hub has been central to innovation at Sodexo. This global innovation platform, available in 14 languages, functions as a marketplace for best practices, idea submissions, and challenges.

By connecting more than 30,000 employees across regions, Innov'Hub fosters collaboration and idea sharing. A flagship initiative of the platform, the 2023 Global Sustainability Challenge, called on employees worldwide to take part in Let's Take A Step Ahead in Sustainability. This initiative gathered over 1,000 ideas, which were assessed by 22 juries globally. Among the winners was Grease to Goodness, an initiative developed by a team in Sodexo Philippines. Recognizing that Sodexo operations in the Philippines produce 23,000 liters of used cooking oil annually, the team proposed repurposing this waste—along with other kitchen waste such as coffee grounds and fruit peels—into soap. Traditionally, this oil is either processed into engine oil or resold to vendors. The soap, an eco-friendly product, is donated to local housing projects, addressing sanitation needs.

Sodexo also cultivates its Open Ecosystem, which is structured around multiple accelerator programs. Since 2017, internal accelerator programs have supported over 15 projects across regions, from Brazil to the United States, with sustainability serving as a selection criterion. The most recent initiative is Sodexo's first Global Accelerator, designed to address challenges faced by its largest global clients. This program has piloted solutions in four countries—France, Israel, Spain, and Singapore—introducing technologies such as dynamic cleaning solutions, paperless digitized routines for operators, and advanced AI applications for CSR data.

In 2024, Sodexo joined the Environmental Startups Accelerator in partnership with Microsoft. This program piloted several solutions, including CircularPlace, a platform to enhance the circularity and reusability of non-food assets. Initially launched in Sodexo France through its innovative "SoTroc" app, CircularPlace has evolved into a client-facing offering. Additionally, Sodexo spearheads annual, theme-driven programs to address pressing challenges. In 2024, the focus on sustainable packaging led to the development of a zero-waste food delivery platform currently being piloted in Sodexo Italia.

By leveraging its global reach, Sodexo ensures that impactful initiatives transition seamlessly from local pilots to global implementation. For instance, Sodexo collaborated with BIBAK, a French technology company specializing in reusable food containers for catering and events. In early 2023, BIBAK secured €6 million in funding to accelerate its development and expand internationally. Working alongside Sodexo has allowed BIBAK to reach corporate clients and deliver its sustainability solutions to a broader audience.

4.2.11 Stellantis—Strategic Convergence Venture Client and CVC

Stellantis, the constellation of 14 automotive brands with operations in more than 30 countries, is leveraging Open Innovation tools under the Tech Division umbrella to fuel both rapid innovation and strategic growth.

Stellantis's Venture Client unit, known as Startup Hub, secures close collaboration with innovative startups to address specific needs identified by Global Functions and Regional Operations. By executing approximately 60 Proof of Concepts (PoCs) per year—of which around one out of three are implemented—selected startups become trusted suppliers, enabling Stellantis to efficiently integrate new innovations across the organization. In 2023, this approach led to signed agreements with 49 new startups with expectations to increase this number by approximately 50% in 2024.

Stellantis Corporate Venture Capital (CVC) arm (Stellantis Ventures) focuses on identifying and investing in startups that align with the group's long-term strategic objectives. The fund, established with an initial allocation of €300 million, targets early and later-stage startup companies that are developing cutting-edge technologies for the automotive and mobility sectors.

Stellantis Venture Studio completes the innovation architecture, leading the global Intrapreneurship program and exploring new business models.

Currently Stellantis is merging the Venture Client (startup collaboration and PoC execution) with the investment activities into a cohesive team with the ultimate goal to streamline the entire innovation process—from identifying internal needs and scouting startups to formalizing commercial contracts and making strategic investments. A recent example of this novel approach is the collaboration with Tiamat, French startup developing Sodium-ion battery chemistry free of lithium and cobalt, holding promise of lower costs, increased sustainability, better low-temperature performances and faster charging capability. Following a PoC, Stellantis and Tiamat entered into a joint development agreement supported by an investment from Stellantis Ventures to explore cost-effective, sustainable alternatives to lithium and cobalt batteries.

4.2.12 TDK—Professionalizing CVC

TDK Ventures, the corporate Venture Capital arm of TDK Corporation, headquartered in Tokyo, Japan, was founded in 2019 by Nicolas Sauvage. Now managing its third fund, TDK Ventures has continually refined and advanced its investment strategies year after year.

TDK Ventures supports technology-driven startups that align with TDK's mission of advancing sustainability through materials science and innovation. With a global presence in Silicon Valley, Boston, London, Bangalore, and Tokyo, TDK Ventures aims at delivering both strategic and financial value. More than just a corporate VC,

TDK Ventures operates with its unique CODE philosophy: Contribute to society, operate as One team reaching for the sky, Deliver deep insights, and put Entrepreneurs first.

TDK Ventures primarily invests in early-stage companies. Aligned with TDK's focus on digital, energy, and environmental transformations, TDK Ventures targets areas such as computing and connectivity, mobility, energy and cleantech, next-gen materials, industrial and robotics, agtech and healthtech. With $350 million in AUM across three funds (two single-LP funds and one multi-LP fund), TDK Ventures' portfolio spans 40 companies, including three unicorns, one IPO, and four M&As. The latest fund, Fund EX1 ($150 million) was launched in June 2023 with a focus on startups in Seed and Series A stage investments in the areas of decarbonization and electrification in Europe and North America.

TDK Ventures collaborates with co-investing partners such as Qualcomm Ventures, Toyota Ventures and Intel Capital. A standout investment is Silicon Box, a Singapore-based unicorn specializing in cutting-edge semiconductor integration services. Another success story is the Massachusetts-based unicorn Ascend Elements, a pioneering company that has developed a novel closed-loop recycling process to recover high-value battery components for reuse.

4.2.13 Unilever—From Corporate-Startup Collaboration to Collaborative Ecosystem Innovation

Established in 2014, Unilever Foundry initially focused on finding solutions for Digital Marketing and eCommerce, particularly in AdTech. Over time, it expanded its scope across all brands, integrating Unilever's Open Innovation activities by connecting internal businesses with startups. In 2022, the Foundry evolved its approach to better align with Unilever's strategic priorities, emphasizing R&D innovation.

The new model focuses on testing and validating innovations before scaling, developing new partnership models, and creating new value rather than just matchmaking. It aims to balance the unique needs of different business groups with the benefits of a unified approach to external engagement. Collaborating with startups, experts and academia in areas like microbiome research, biotechnology, material chemistry and AI-driven R&D, the Foundry has created a structured innovation path. The process encompasses four stages: Scoping (defining business challenges), Sourcing (identifying and partnering with global innovators), Validating (assessing viability), and Scaling (integrating solutions into the core business).

This year the Foundry celebrates its 10th anniversary. With a decade of experience in collaborative innovation, they recognize that "today's challenges cannot be solved through a single corporate-startup collaboration. Big issues like net zero, regenerative agriculture and the reduction of plastic in packaging lack a single owner and require multiple partners". The Foundry has enhanced its capacity for validating and scaling solutions, transforming into a strategic enabler within Unilever. By combining Unilever's domain expertise with collaborators' creativity, they've empowered teams across the business and set new standards for innovation and sustainability. The Foundry now plays a central role in driving business transformation, with teams based in the USA, UK, Netherlands, China, and India.

Since its inception, the Foundry has facilitated over 400 strategic collaborations. One notable example is its partnership with Unilever's One Packaging Team to develop sustainable flexible packaging. The team aimed to find biodegradable, recyclable materials with high barrier properties—a challenging combination. Through the Foundry's global network, they connected with startups working on alternative barrier technologies, reducing the proof-of-concept testing timeline from six months to just two.

The Foundry co-leads Unilever's participation in the 100+ Accelerator, a program launched in 2018 to address global sustainability challenges. This initiative, led by Unilever, AB InBev, Coca Cola, Colgate-Palmolive, and Danone, selects around 30 startups each year to collaborate on projects ranging from biodiversity and water stewardship to inclusive growth. One of the five startups selected for a 2024 pilot is GluECO, a bio-based adhesive innovator. GluECO will test a heat sealant made from corn protein and other bio-based ingredients for paper packaging, with a pilot also running with Colgate-Palmolive.

The Unilever Foundry has transformed into a strategic innovation enabler, driving sustainable solutions through collaborative partnerships. By tackling global challenges with a collaborative ecosystem approach, it sets new standards for innovation and sustainability within Unilever.

4.2.14 Volvo—CampX Interconnected Innovation Model

Launched in Gothenburg in 2019, CampX by Volvo Group is a strategic engine to boost transformation through partnerships with innovative startups.

Started in Sweden and later on extended to India, France and the US, CampX is strategically located near key Volvo Group Research & Development sites to facilitate close collaboration with production and business lines. The core team comprises 16 full-time employees, supported by cross-functional teams from legal, intellectual property, purchasing and essential product and business stakeholders. When the Volvo Group's product and business owners identify a challenge, the CampX team swiftly launches a Proof of Value project. In a large corporation, failing fast requires a culture of trust, and CampX aims to foster exactly this environment.

The CampX Innovation model consists of three engagement programs tailored for each phase of the startup's journey: an Incubator, a Venture Client and a Venture Builder program. The Incubator nurtures early-stage startups and ventures, offering access to Volvo Group engineers and facilities. Since the first batch in 2023, CampX has supported ten early phase startups and one alumnus.

The Venture Client program focuses on short demand-driven innovation projects, facilitating co-creation through Proof of Value setups. Up-to-date there are 100 projects in the portfolio worldwide and 9 launched to date as well as 12 in the pipe for launch activities.

The Venture Builder generates new revenue streams by capitalizing on internal business opportunities and intellectual property within the sustainable mobility ecosystem. This has already produced two spinouts, Fyrqom and Cetasol, with several additional projects in the pipeline. Startups can "travel" between programs based on their needs, with several quickly transitioning from the Incubator to the Venture Client. For instance, Fyrqom was created in the Venture Builder, developing an automated workflow for tire-related activities, transitioned to the Venture Client for Proof of Value and is now in the Incubator, conducting pilots across Volvo Group factories. The CampX concept operates as a highly autonomous "vehicle" on its own. Following a 3–6 month Proof of Value, if the product owner determines it effective, CampX remains open to explore further collaboration—either through partnership and co-development or potentially by licensing or acquisition.

4.2.15 A2A—CVC Backed by VC

A2A launched its Corporate Venture Capital (CVC) activities in 2020 with "360LIFE I", a fund managed by 360 Capital, where A2A acted as the sole Limited Partner (LP). Since then, A2A has expanded its strategy to include participation in technology transfer funds, fostering spinouts focused on sustainability, deep tech, and advanced materials. Recently, A2A introduced a successor fund, "360LIFE II", also managed by 360 Capital.

What sets A2A's approach to CVC apart is its gradual and evolving strategy. With "360LIFE I", A2A chose to outsource the management of investment activities to 360 Capital, while an A2A professional was seconded to the fund. This initial €25 million allocation resulted in investments in eight European startups. With the new fund, "360LIFE II", A2A has increased its total commitment to approximately €80 million. Unlike its predecessor, this second fund is open to external LPs, including institutional, financial, and industrial players. A2A will also take on a more active role in managing the fund: the investment team now includes professionals from both 360 Capital and A2A.

Specifically, A2A will handle technical due diligence and work to establish industrial synergies through proofs of concept (PoCs) and commercial partnerships with its business units. Another notable aspect is the opportunity for A2A employees involved in the fund's activities to participate in the carry—a feature that is relatively uncommon in the corporate sector. A2A's CVC activities are primarily strategic in nature. The company has established partnerships with all its portfolio companies. A prime example is the UK-based startup Greyparrot, which developed cutting-edge computer vision and robotic solutions for waste management. This technology was successfully piloted at A2A's plastic recycling facility in Milan in 2021 and later scaled through A2A's Business Unit.

4.3 Signals Reshaping the Open Innovation Arena

The case studies above illustrate initiatives spanning Venture Client, CVC, Venture Builders, Accelerators, and Intrapreneurship, while also highlighting the enabling factors (strategy, organization, culture, and processes) that determine whether Open Innovation delivers measurable results and value.

Companies are increasingly mastering and refining their preferred Open Innovation models. TDK has achieved excellence in CVC, while Bosch (both at group level and through BSH Home Appliances Group) exemplifies leadership in the Venture Client model. Others, such as 3M, Siemens, and EDF, are strengthening existing approaches by integrating additional tools like Venture Building. A visible trend is the externalization of innovation vehicles to create organizational separation and enable specialized management, as seen with Olam (Venture Building) and A2A (CVC). Hybrid strategies are also emerging: Stellantis and Maersk combine Venture Client with CVC, while ACCIONA is shifting its focus from startup acceleration toward investment and M&A.

Open Innovation is increasingly tied to broader agendas such as sustainability and local development, as demonstrated by Japan Airlines and Sodexo. Repsol and Volvo Group highlight the importance of holistic approaches that align multiple Open Innovation models under a unified strategic vision. Similarly, Unilever illustrates the evolution from isolated corporate-startup collaborations toward ecosystem-driven innovation. At its most advanced stage, Open Innovation reshapes corporate strategy itself.

In conclusion, the landscape of Open Innovation is not merely evolving but being continuously redefined. The cases presented here show that success depends on treating Open Innovation as a dynamic, adaptive process capable of responding to changing technologies and markets. The growing adoption of hybrid, inclusive, and strategically embedded models positions Open Innovation as a cornerstone of sustainable growth and long-term competitive advantage. Looking ahead, companies that internalize these lessons and adopt multifaceted strategies will be best positioned to drive innovation and shape the industries of the future.

References

Mind the Bridge. (2024). The open innovation imperative: Adapting to stay competitive—Evolve or be extinct season 2024. https://mindthebridge.com/the-open-innovation-imperative-adapting-to-stay-competitive-evolve-or-be-extinct-season-2024/

Mind the Bridge. (2025). Open innovation outlook 2025—Trends for 2025 in corporate startup engagement. https://mindthebridge.com/open-innovation-outlook-2025-trends-for-2025-in-corporate-startup-engagement/

Chapter 5
Measuring Open Innovation Impact

Abstract Many firms are now implementing Open Innovation. However, measuring the value generated by Open Innovation initiatives remains a challenge. On the one hand, many initiatives deliver impact only in the medium to long term. On the other, most of the benefits are intangible and often difficult, if not impossible, to quantify. A clear understanding of the mechanisms—both internal and external—that determine when and how companies can fully capture value from Open Innovation is still lacking. So far, only preliminary approaches to measurement systems and key performance indicators have been developed, underlining the need for more robust frameworks to assess and maximize the true impact of Open Innovation.

Keywords Metrics · KPI · Evaluation · Impact

5.1 KPIs and the Impact on Firms Financial Performance

In the early days of Open Innovation, many established companies were more focused on showcasing their involvement with startups than on genuinely co-innovating with them—a phase sometimes described as the "Age of Marketing" (Mind the Bridge, 2023). Today, however, the emphasis has shifted toward tangible collaborations and measurable economic impact, making clear KPIs and reliable data essential (Fig. 5.1). This evolution has intensified the search for effective ways to assess the true value of Open Innovation.

Both scholars and practitioners have long sought to develop metrics to measure Open Innovation and its impact on organizations and society (Lu & Chesbrough, 2022). Yet researching Open Innovation metrics remains challenging due to the diversity of contexts, the wide range of organizations adopting them (Brunswicker & Chesbrough, 2018), and the heterogeneity of Open Innovation practices.

Despite the growing attention of corporates to metrics, empirical studies examining the impact of Open Innovation on firm performance have produced mixed results (Cobben & Bogers, 2024; Lu & Chesbrough, 2022), often constrained by methodological limitations. Much of the existing research relies on survey or archival

A. Onetti and A. Pisoni, *Open Innovation in Action*,
SpringerBriefs in Entrepreneurship and Innovation,
https://doi.org/10.1007/978-3-032-17332-4_5

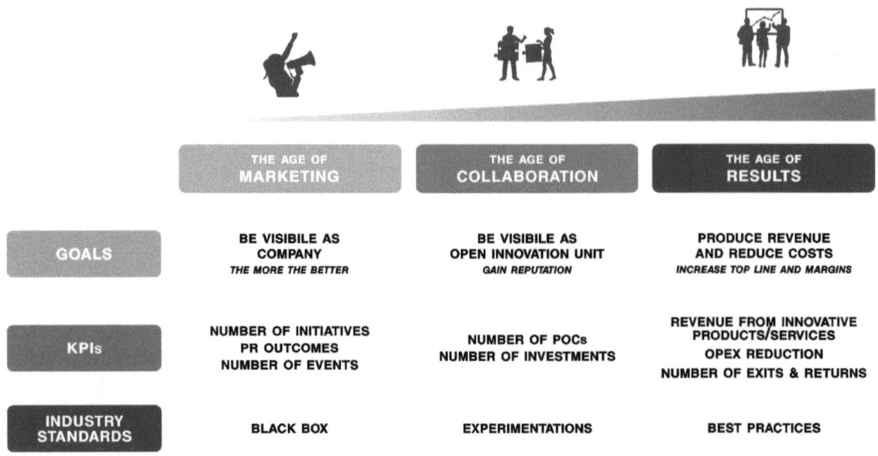

Fig. 5.1 The ages of Open Innovation. *Source* Own elaboration adapted from Mind the Bridge (2023)

data, typically conducted in isolation or aggregated through proxies. Moreover, linking Open Innovation to firm-level financial performance is inherently difficult, as Open Innovation is a broad and multifaceted concept encompassing multiple practices (Brunswicker & Chesbrough, 2018; Chesbrough, 2003). In other words, the relationship between Open Innovation practices and financial performance varies significantly by practice and sector (Lu & Chesbrough, 2022).

As discussed in the previous chapters, the main value drivers associated with Open Innovation include the provision of strategic market intelligence and the opportunity for diversification into adjacent or entirely new markets. Open Innovation also supports cultural transformation by reintroducing an entrepreneurial mindset across the organization, an attitude that often gradually fades as firms evolve from their initial startup phase into more operation-focused structures. In addition, Open Innovation enhances corporate branding and reputation, reinforcing the company's positioning as an innovative actor while reducing its overall financial risk profile. A persistent challenge, however, is that these impacts are largely intangible and difficult to track and measure through conventional metrics or KPIs in the short to medium term.

Assessing the financial and economic outcomes of Open Innovation initiatives is inherently complex, as their tangible effects typically emerge only over extended time horizons (see Chapter 3; Mind the Bridge, 2023). In today's climate of growing economic uncertainty, however, measuring and clearly communicating their impact has become essential. While Open Innovation initiatives primarily drive strategic and cultural transformations—largely intangible in nature—their economic and financial outcomes, though more tangible, generally surface only in the medium to long term (Fig. 5.2).

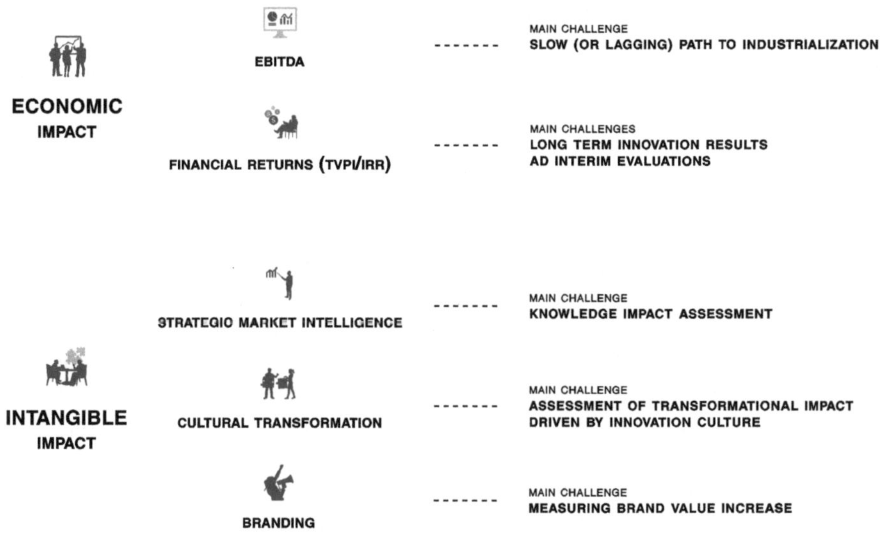

Fig. 5.2 Open Innovation impacts and related challenges. *Source* Own elaboration adapted from Mind the Bridge (2023)

The impact of Open Innovation on corporate performance also varies significantly depending on the tools adopted. Empirical evidence from practice highlights the following patterns:

- **Venture Client**: Value generated through collaborations with startups—reflected in the Income Statement (P&L) and EBITDA—typically materializes only after the pilot or PoC phase has been completed, and solutions are scaled into industrial adoption (Mind the Bridge, 2023). Quantifying these benefits remains challenging, particularly when it comes to measuring reduced time-to-market and the integration of new revenue streams into existing offerings (Fig. 5.2).
- **Corporate Venture Capital (CVC)**: Financial returns usually appear over an 8–10-year horizon, coinciding with portfolio exits. Interim evaluations are therefore unreliable. Common indicators such as Total Value to Paid-In Capital (TVPI) tend to fluctuate widely, and residual values remain highly unpredictable.
- **Venture Builders**: Still in their infancy (Fig. 5.2), venture builders lack the maturity to consistently report concrete financial results, rendering current assessments largely speculative. A further challenge is their focus on a limited number of selective, idiosyncratic internal ventures, which makes evaluation even more complex.
- **Corporate Accelerators**: These programs have generally shown limited effectiveness, with outcomes often failing to justify operational costs. Unsurprisingly, many corporations have already discontinued them or are considering doing so.

More broadly, the benefits that Open Innovation provides in terms of market insights, strategic contributions, and reputational gains remain even more difficult to quantify, even though they play a critical role in shaping long-term competitiveness.

5.2 Challenges Related to Measurement

Several scholars have emphasized the need for further research on the operationalization and implementation of Open Innovation metrics, as existing measures often fall short of practitioners' needs and frequently lack validity (Audretsch & Belitski, 2023; Cobben & Bogers, 2024; Dabić et al., 2023). The increasing openness of innovation systems adds to the challenge, as projects are often characterized by significant technical and market uncertainty. The adoption of Open Innovation practices may also involve risks (Frishammar et al., 2015; Marullo et al., 2020), such as the "paradox of openness" (Laursen & Salter, 2014), whereby the benefits of opening up must be carefully balanced against the risk of knowledge leakage. In such contexts, firms are "playing poker rather than chess" (Chesbrough, 2003, 2024), meaning they need evaluation metrics that account for external sources and alternative exploitation paths of innovation.

Ideally, practitioners require clear, easy-to-use Open Innovation metrics that provide actionable insights. As recent research highlights, integrating the practitioners' perspective is essential for developing metrics that are directly usable (Cobben & Bogers, 2024). Such metrics should be forward-looking and responsive, enabling timely interventions when necessary. However, most current Open Innovation metrics are backward-looking and often fail to capture what they are designed to measure. The challenge, therefore, is to create metrics that meet practical needs while remaining rigorous and adaptable.

Improving Open Innovation measurement requires collaboration between academia and industry. The first step is to map what needs to be measured, identify existing metrics, and uncover the gaps. The next step is to validate new metrics in their specific application contexts to ensure relevance and accuracy. Metrics should be understandable, up-to-date, and able to provide a clear picture of the current situation. Organizations should also continuously assess the relevance and effectiveness of their Open Innovation metrics to ensure alignment with evolving practices and goals.

In conclusion, effective Open Innovation metrics are essential to legitimize the contributions of both academics and practitioners, and to assess the impact of Open Innovation on corporate performance. Given the persistent difficulties in measuring the benefits of Open Innovation, firms face inevitable trade-offs when selecting metrics. Scholars and practitioners must therefore carefully define the contexts, practices, and impacts they aim to capture in order to ensure the effectiveness of Open Innovation measurement.

References

Audretsch, D., & Belitski, M. (2023). The limits to open innovation and its impact on innovation performance. *Technovation, 119*, Article 102519. https://doi.org/10.1016/j.technovation.2022.102519

Brunswicker, S., & Chesbrough, H. (2018). The adoption of Open Innovation in large firms: Practices, measures, and risks a survey of large firms examines how firms approach open innovation strategically and manage knowledge flows at the project level. *Research-Technology Management, 61*(1), 35–45. https://doi.org/10.1080/08956308.2018.1399022

Chesbrough, H. (2003). *Open innovation: The new imperative for creating and profiting from technology*. Harvard Business Press.

Chesbrough, H. (2024). A reconsideration of Open Innovation after 20 years. In H. Chesbrough, A. Radziwon, W. Vanhaverbeke, & J. West (Eds.), *The Oxford handbook of open innovation* (pp. 3–18). Oxford University Press.

Cobben, D., & Bogers, M. (2024). The use of open innovation metrics. In H. Chesbrough, A. Radziwon, W. Vanhaverbeke, & J. West (Eds.), *The Oxford handbook of open innovation* (pp. 869–884). Oxford University Press.

Dabić, M., Daim, T., Bogers, M. L., & Mention, A. L. (2023). The limits of open innovation: Failures, risks, and costs in open innovation practice and theory. *Technovation, 126*, Article 102786. https://doi.org/10.1016/j.technovation.2023.102786

Frishammar, J., Ericsson, K., & Patel, P. C. (2015). The dark side of knowledge transfer: Exploring knowledge leakage in joint R&D projects. *Technovation, 41*, 75–88. https://doi.org/10.1016/j.technovation.2015.01.001

Laursen, K., & Salter, A. J. (2014). The paradox of openness: Appropriability, external search and collaboration. *Research Policy, 43*(5), 867–878. https://doi.org/10.1016/j.respol.2013.10.004

Lu, Q., & Chesbrough, H. (2022). Measuring open innovation practices through topic modelling: Revisiting their impact on firm financial performance. *Technovation, 114*, Article 102434. https://doi.org/10.1016/j.technovation.2021.102434

Marullo, C., Di Minin, A., De Marco, C., & Piccaluga, A. (2020). Is open innovation always the best for SMEs? An exploratory analysis at the project level. *Creativity and Innovation Management, 29*(2), 209–223. https://doi.org/10.1111/caim.12375

Mind the Bridge. (2023). Open Innovation: The age of hybridization and results—Evolve or be extinct. https://mindthebridge.com/2023-open-innovation-evolve-or-be-extinct/

Chapter 6
Conclusions and Future Outlook

Abstract Open Innovation has become a mainstream approach reshaping industries worldwide. As technology evolves at unprecedented speed, no company can master all critical expertise internally. Startups and scaleups now serve as agile innovation partners, accelerating disruptive breakthroughs and offering corporates new pathways to growth. This book explores how established firms are embracing Open Innovation to enhance adaptability, creativity, and competitiveness. Data insights, and case studies reveal that successful Open Innovation is not a static formula but a dynamic, hybrid process integrating strategy, culture, and measurement. Companies that learn from best practices and continuously evolve their collaboration models will lead industry transformation, while those that fail to adapt risk obsolescence.

Keywords Adaptability · Flexibility · Hybrid innovation models

Open Innovation has become mainstream, expanding across industries and geographies. The accelerating pace and growing complexity of technological change make it nearly impossible for any company—regardless of sector, geography, or size—to master all relevant expertise in-house. Startups and scaleups have emerged as the new "innovation vessels", fast, agile speedboats driving disruptive breakthroughs that are reshaping markets and dethroning incumbents. Yet whether they turn out to be torpedoes or lifeboats depends on how the world's big corporate tankers choose to engage with them.

Whether by choice or necessity, an increasing number of established companies are embracing Open Innovation and collaborating with startups, tapping into their innovation pool to avoid missed opportunities and enhance adaptability, flexibility, and creativity. Startups are no longer seen only as potential disruptors, but as catalysts for corporate innovation, enabling partnerships that create mutual value and fuel growth.

Over the past decade, the Open Innovation landscape has not just evolved—it has been fundamentally redefined. Corporate-led initiatives have expanded in scope and sophistication. As shown in Chapter 3, research on corporate-startup collaboration

A. Onetti and A. Pisoni, *Open Innovation in Action*,
SpringerBriefs in Entrepreneurship and Innovation,
https://doi.org/10.1007/978-3-032-17332-4_6

now focuses on the models and strategies companies adopt and the factors behind successful partnerships.

The data, insights, and case studies presented in this book highlight a clear trend: successful Open Innovation is not a static, one-size-fits-all formula but a dynamic process that adapts to shifting technologies, market demands, and competitive pressures. Observing top-performing companies reveals valuable lessons—not only in what they do, but in how they have continuously evolved their approaches. Chapter 4 illustrates this through diverse initiatives such as Venture Client models, CVC, Venture Builders, Accelerators, and Intrapreneurship, framed within broader considerations of strategy, organization, culture, and processes. Collectively, the evidence shows how leading firms are progressively moving toward hybrid, integrated approaches.

As the Open Innovation field advances, one truth becomes evident: companies that embrace this evolution, learn from best practices, adopt multifaceted strategies, and track results (Chapter 5) will be best positioned to lead industry transformation. For the others, the risk is existential. Evolve or be extinct.

MIX
Papier aus verantwortungsvollen Quellen
Paper from responsible sources
FSC® C105338

If you have any concerns about our products,
you can contact us on
ProductSafety@springernature.com

In case Publisher is established outside the EU,
the EU authorized representative is:
Springer Nature Customer Service Center GmbH
Europaplatz 3, 69115 Heidelberg, Germany

Printed by Libri Plureos GmbH
in Hamburg, Germany